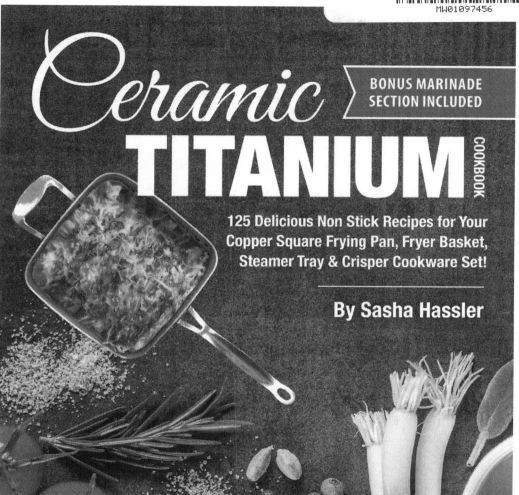

Ceramic TITANIUM COOKBOOK

BONUS MARINADE SECTION INCLUDED

125 Delicious Non Stick Recipes for Your Copper Square Frying Pan, Fryer Basket, Steamer Tray & Crisper Cookware Set!

By Sasha Hassler

Sasha Hassler & Allison August

HLR Press
Southern California

LEGAL NOTICE

WANT FREE BOOKS? JUST SAY YES!

OUR NEW BOOKS SENT TO YOUR EMAIL MONTHLY

For our current readers...if you like receiving free books to add to your collection, then this is for you! This is for promoting our material to our current members so you can review our new books and give us feed back when we launch new books we are publishing! This helps us determine how we can make our books better for you, our audience! Just go to the url below and leave your name and email. We will send you a complimentary book about once a month. And just an fyi...on the website we've posted a few videos for you here too...

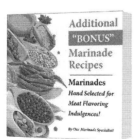

"Additional Marinades"

Yours FREE for signing up to Our List!

www.Healthylifestylerecipes.Org/Freebook2review

INTRODUCTION

This book will show you why this safe non stick cookware is the only set you should have in your kitchen to cook with! If you've recently purchased a non stick copper ceramic titanium skillet, frying pan or any of its accessories, then this book can quickly give you the expertise you need to fully enjoy the benefits of non stick cuisine. This book was written for today's reader with quick, short paragraphs. There are also plenty of illustrations and easy-to-understand instructions. And, with 99 delicious and popular recipes at your fingertips, you'll always have a healthy meal ready for guests and family. In this book you will also learn: how to choose the best non stick skillet. How to clean your non stick cookware and take care of it, a history of non-stick pan cookware, pro-tips to help you excel in the kitchen and over 125 popular and deliciously healthy recipes to choose from!

We also have a little surprise for you...we've got recipes for the crisper, fry basket, steamer, square pan and round pan! So you can use this book for pretty much anything that has to do with cooking! Also included in this book...a new "bonus section" for mouth watering marinades! So if you want your meat to be this amazingly "high flavored, smack in the mouth" taste that you've never experienced before...then we have "this bonus section" for you to enjoy! These are our 10 favorite marinades that we pulled out of "our play book" just for you! Every pulsating taste of bliss that you'll every want on your meats is right here at your fingertips!

"Now it's time to impress, not only your peers, but yourself with these delicious, unique recipes and meat soaking, mouth watering marinades!"

Enjoy!

Sasha & Allison xoxo

TABLE OF CONTENTS

CHAPTER 1:
WHY THIS BOOK IS GOOD
FOR YOUR KITCHEN

IT'S THE ONLY INSTRUCTIONAL BOOK MADE FOR THE CERAMIC TITANIUM SQUARE PAN & ACCESSORIES

There are many books that have been created for different types of recipes and even cookware. When you browse the magazine aisles at the supermarket or the cooking section at your local book store, you find quite a few books that are catered for grills, bbqs and slow cookers. However, this is the only book that has been written for our ceramic titanium square pan.

WHY DOES THIS PAN NEED ITS OWN BOOK?

Because it's one of a kind! This type of pan is the pan of all pans. Once you purchase a pan like this, you will learn that it is the only pan that you will ever need. Every chapter in this book is perfectly crafted and laid out for this pan. You will find everything that you need to know about this fry pan in this book and by the time you are done, you will tell all your friends.

OVER 125 UNIQUE & MOUTHWATERING RECIPES!

These recipe book was made for anyone with any type of copper round pan, square pan, fry basket, steamer tray or crisper! Every recipe in this book was handpicked for this ceramic titanium pan set and its many uses. You will not find one recipe that you cannot use with this pan, which is another way to show you why it is the best. From meats and pastas to breakfast and desserts, our ceramic titanium square pan will wow you. You're strapped for time and need something to whip up in 20 minutes or less, or you're in the mood for steak and potatoes. You can create these fun filled and romantic dinners in our ceramic titanium square pan, and much more.

ELITE RECIPES THAT MAKE YOU LOOK LIKE A PRO

From beginners, to world-renowned chefs, our ceramic titanium square pan and the accessories are super easy to use, clean and even store. For those who are new to the world of cooking, our ceramic titanium square pan and these accessories should be your go to cookware of choice. You can make "one skillet meals" in here that will have your friends and family cheering and in no time you can brush up on your cooking skills.

With the unique recipes that we have picked just for this pan, you can become the type of cook that you want to be. (these products are so versatile that you can learn to pan fry, oven roast and sauté, bake, basket fry, steam and oven crisp your food just like any professional you've seen on tv and even one that would make your grandmother proud.)

HEALTHIEST WAY TO COOK TO LOWER CHOLESTEROL

The greatest thing about our ceramic titanium square pan and its accessories is that they are "super non-stick". Unlike most other pans, steamers, fry baskets and crispers, they do not require any fat or butter to keep food from sticking, flaking or breaking onto the pan. **Note:** if you do find that the pan sticks a little, just put a dab of oil on a paper towel and wipe the pan. It's that simple! (a professional chef's trick of the trade!) Again, adding oils is not a must anymore but a choice...for flavor that is. This is important because all of that butter and fat could cause a person to have very high cholesterol. This ceramic titanium cookbook is the healthier choice and helps lower your cholesterol one meal at a time.

"TOSS THOSE OLD PANS…"

THIS IS THE ONLY NON-STICK PAN YOU'LL EVER NEED!

Round pan or square pan…this is virtually the only non-stick pan that you will ever need. The non-stick ceramic titanium coating is teflon, ptfe, and pfoa free and thus allows your food to slide off with ease, without the health risks that come with it. You can cook a variety of food on the pan, even spaghetti, and do not have to worry if you need to put it in the oven to cook meals. This pan are so versatile that you can heat it up to 850º f and even throw that "bad boy" in the dishwasher for a safe clean. However, if you want to go old fashioned, you can clean it off with a rag and store it next to all your other pans, without worrying about the pan getting scratched or ruined. Why wouldn't you want to add this great pan to you or a loved one's cooking collection?

CHAPTER 2:
WHAT'S SO SPECIAL ABOUT THIS PAN?

ULTRA-DURABLE AND SCRATCH-RESISTANT

For this pan we have done our own unofficial analysis to put this thing to the test but do not recommend you do this. You know...shopping for a pan can be a pretty important task. After all, you are going to be cooking all of your food in this one or set of pans. So, you better make a good choice right? There are so many kinds to choose from. How do you choose the best one for you? Well, for starters, you want a pan that will last a long time. I know that i would be furious if i bought a pan and had to throw it away within a couple of months because of scratches and the fact that the coating was starting to peel off. How unhealthy and unsanitary is that?

Well, i will be the first to tell you that this ceramic titanium pan is the best investment that you will ever make. Ceramic titanium is a lightweight metal coating and one of the strongest to be exact. The pan has a type of coating that makes it scratch resistant, which means that you can use utensils on the base of the pan and it will not scratch or peel the surface. The other great thing about this pan is that it will never corrode or rust on you! "now that's a pan you want in your kitchen!"

IT'S LIKE COOKING ON AIR...
FOOD SLIDES RIGHT OUT OF THE PAN!

You have all your ingredients ready, but you are out of oil or butter, or you are trying to lose weight, but you need to coat the pan with butter or oil so the food doesn't stick. What do you do? There is no need to worry because this ceramic titanium pan is super non-stick. This means that the food you cook with it doesn't need any oil or butter. You can cook everything you need without it. It's that simple! You will actually feel like you are cooking on air because all of the food slides right out and onto the plate.

100% SAFE: PFOA, AND PTFE-FREE

We are all aware of the danger of teflon style non-stick pans. This is the brand that often gives non-stick pans a bad reputation because they can cause many different types of health issues. First of all, teflon is a type of coating that is owned by the dupont company. Teflon coating is often fluoropolymer plastic (ptfe), perfluoroctanoic acid (pfoa) based. These chemicals are very harmful and can cause consumers to get very sick.

So, how can you tell if the pan that you are looking for is safe? Well...this is one if the safest pans you can buy on the market by my opinion! This non-stick ceramic titanium pan does not contain these harmful chemicals! The lack of these chemicals make this product much safer for consumers and you can go about your cooking knowing that your health is safe!

DISHWASHER SAFE

After a long day of cooking, the last thing anyone wants to do is clean up the kitchen. Thank god for your dishwasher right? Wrong. Didn't you read that you couldn't put your non-stick pan into the dishwasher and you had to refrain from certain soaps and other types of cleaners because they might ruin the surface of the pan and cause it to erode? Well, you can scratch that. Remember how the pan is scratch resistant, well; it is dishwasher safe as well. Most non-stick pans have a problem with dealing with high heats and this is the reason that you cannot put them in the dishwasher. This is not the case with the non-stick pan. If you can put them in the oven, they would be able to survive the dishwasher, leaving you more time to do what you want and less time cleaning up the kitchen.

CHAPTER 3:
NON-STICK CERAMIC TITANIUM BENEFITS!

THE HEALTHIEST CHOICE IN COOKING

We live in an age where people are starting to be more health conscious. We see this in everything that we do, from ads on tv to what we read in magazines. Why would our cookware be any different? This is where we cook the food that goes into our bodies. So, of course this is going to be important to us. Most of the food that we cook requires oils and butter so that it does not stick to the pan.

Well, we no longer need to worry about that. This non-stick ceramic titanium pan requires no oils or butters. The non-stick coating that is on the base of the pan keeps foods from sticking. That's the whole purpose of the pan, but it is a major health benefit to us. Of course we need some oils or fat to help our skin, this is where a little bit of olive or avocado oil can be used for some flavor. Just remember that this is not an essential ingredient for cooking anymore, rather a choice.

CAN WITHSTAND HIGH LEVELS OF HEAT UP TO 850º

You're cooking with your non-stick pan and the recipe calls for putting the ingredients into the oven. So, what do you do? Do you transfer your ingredients to an oven safe dish? The answer is no. This ceramic titanium non-stick pan is oven safe and can withhold heat up to 850º f. This is great. The whole dish isn't ruined and you don't have to worry about your pan as well. These are things that all types of cooks care about; preserving the life of their pan and saving the dish. After all, what is more important?

THE MOST VERSATILE OF COOKWARE

Cast iron skillets and pans have been the top choice, as far as cookware durability and strength. However, it seems that ceramic titanium has taken its place. Ceramic titanium is just as durable as cast iron, in my opinion and is lighter as well. This is a huge advantage because you don't need a workout to pick up and move the pan, like you did the cast iron skillet. Campers have found that the ceramic titanium pan is so much better than tin, which is what they have previously used. Tin is flimsy, flexible and can dent easily. It does not have the durability and versatility of ceramic titanium .

Some of the great advantages of using a ceramic titanium non-stick pan is that it contains quick heating metal, and a stainless steel induction plate to make sure your pan heats up fast. This means that you cannot only put the pan in the broiler or the oven, but that it is dishwasher safe as well. When placed on the stove, it does heat much faster than other pans of the same size. Since the pan can heat up to high temperatures, it can serve as its own stove. This is another reason why campers tend to use the pan for all of their cooking needs.

NON-ALLERGENIC AND ANTIBACTERIAL

Staying healthy is a huge priority in the kitchen. This theme is universal when prepping/preparing and even cleaning up our food. And the theme stretches as far as what types of cookware that we are using. There are many arguments on why non-stick titanium/ceramic pans are the best, but this reason is the icing on the cake. When cooking, there are many rules on how we are supposed to clean our surfaces, and cookware, as well as store them. Well, the titanium/ceramic non-stick pan has one up on most of the other non-stick and stick pans. **What is that? You say.** Well, this pan set can be used by mostly anyone because not only are they so versatile but they are nonreactive, nonporous, non-allergenic and they are also anti-bacterial. So, you do not have to worry about germs. These pans can be cleaned by being wiped down by a rag or a cloth and stored away for the next use. That's how i clean mine and it's quick and easy!

EASY TO CLEAN AND STORE

Keeping proper care of your non-stick pans is very important. This can ensure that you keep using the pan for a very long time. One of the ways to do this is to keep your pan clean for best quality performance. Any food residue or leftover grease can actually cook onto the surface of the pan, which can actually cause food to stick and defeat the whole purpose of a non-stick pan. Leaving leftover food or residue on the pan can be hard to detect. Just make sure that you wipe the pan out clean or wash the pan thoroughly every time.

It is also important to store the pan properly to preserve its lifespan and performance. Some manufacturers sometimes suggest that you hang your pan on either a hanging rack or something that will give the same effect. This leaves room between each pan or pot, thus illuminating acquiring some residue or grease that may have been left on others. This also allows the pan room to breathe. I know this sounds funny, but even pans need fresh air. If you do not have a hanging rack, then it is okay to store the pan in a cabinet or in other areas where you store your personal cookware!

CHAPTER 4:

A HISTORY OF THE NON-STICK PAN

TECHNOLOGY THAT IS OLD AS THE ANCIENT GREEKS?

Non-stick cookware sounds like a new type of invention right? Well, at least something that was created in the 19th or 20th century at least. The idea is over 2,000 years old. Due to an archaeology site found near naples, archaeologists have determined that romans used non-stick pans too. The problem of food sticking to pots must have frustrated them as well. Some of the pottery that was discovered was coated with a red, slippery coating that was determined to keep stews from sticking to the bottom of pots. How exciting is that?

The ancient mycenaean's (greeks) also used non-stick cookware to help preserve their bread. The greeks used griddles to cook their bread and found that the dough was sticky and tended to burn onto the top of the griddles. There were two sides to the griddle, a smooth side and a side with holes. The bread was more than likely going to stick on the smooth surface of the griddle. However, the holes were actually an ancient non-stick secret. The holes ensured that the oil spread evenly over the surface of the griddle. So, now we know that ancient greeks and romans were trying to find ways to cook better and easier.

DUPONT'S DISCOVERY OF TEFLON

Did you know that teflon was actually invented by accident? Roy plunkett, a dupont chemist, invented teflon when he was trying to make a better refrigerator. The chemist decided to combine the gas form of tetrafluoroethylene with hydrochloric acid. When he gathered the gas, he pressurized and cooled it in canisters overnight. When he returned the next day, the gas was gone. Plunkett couldn't understand what happened because the gas weighed the same as they did the night before.

Plunkett decided to cut the canisters in half and noticed that the gas had hardened on all sides, creating a type of slick surface. Instead of throwing the canisters away, he and his assistant tested the new substance and found that it was extremely slippery, as well as inactive to all chemicals. This was an amazing find, but some of the best things are created by accident.

FROM AEROSPACE TO COOKWARE

The creation of teflon had nothing to do with cooking. That came about by accident as well. However, when plunkett trademarked teflon in 1945, it was picked up by the military and used as a type of artillery shell and in the construction of nuclear material for many projects, particularly the manhattan project. Marc gregoire, a french engineer who worked at a french aerospace research agency (onera) used teflon to remove glass fiber molds. When his wife heard about this, she challenged him to create a type of nonstick cookware by adding teflon to the base of aluminum pans. Thus, teflon nonstick pans were made. A company known as tefal decided to market this cooking invention and made it an international success. This invention has helped us find ways to cook our food in a much healthier way.

HOW NON-STICK PANS ARE MADE

If non-stick pans are unique and special, shouldn't they be specially made? Well, they are. There is a specific chemical recipe that needs to be followed in order to ensure that the pan is going to do what it was meant to do. Like keep things from sticking, which eliminates the use of butters and oils; essentially creating a healthier way for us to cook our food and watch our calorie intake. The process starts with a ladle machine that creates a mold of melted aluminum, which makes the base of pans. The excess is then cut off and the pan is moved to a spot where a flame melts a series of powders onto the pan to give it that ceramic coating that we have grown to know and love. When referring to the ceramic titanium pan for the newer style skillets...there is another process involved but these are the basics of the non-stick pan and how they are made and have come into existence! **"things that make you go...hmmmmmm..."**

CHAPTER 5:

HOW TO USE YOUR NON-STICK CERAMIC TITANIUM SET

THIS NON-STICK SET WILL TRANSFORM YOUR COOKING

Tired of your same old pots and pans? Tired of the scrubbing, the scratches and the coating that comes off and changes the taste of your food and ends up in your mouth? For starters, those who have a busy schedule can use it to create dishes they never thought possible, in the same pan and in under 30 minutes.

However, with all of the recipes that we provide in this book, you are able to grow from just a beginner to the person grandma is calling to bring dessert to the next family holiday or get together. ;) this pan is every cooks dream because it is so easy to use that it takes all the worry out of cooking. Before you know it, you will be dying to get into the kitchen and cooking all of those healthy meals that you never dreamed of making before.

NO OIL! NO BUTTER! OH MY!

I'm sure the whole reason behind the creation of these non-stick pans was to make cooking easier and healthier. No one likes their food sticking to the pan, but who wants to use all that oil and butter? We all know that it's tradition to throw in a teaspoon of butter or oil to the pan and let it melt before cooking, but sometimes it's okay to break away from that tradition and create your own. With non-stick pans you can make your own tradition and start cooking without butter or oils, unless you choose to use them for flavor. **Note:** if you do find that the pan sticks a little, just put a dab of oil on a paper towel and wipe the pan. It's that simple! Believe me; your health will thank us.

USING METAL UTENSILS IS SAFE!

We all have read the warnings about non-stick pans and metal. They tell us to shy away from metal because these utensils can scratch the surface. So, you put your metal spatula away and started using that flimsy plastic one. And, you hate it. Well, with the ceramic non-stick titanium frying pan, you can retire that plastic spatula forever and start using the metal one again, because these pans are scratch proof. That's right. You heard me. The ceramic titanium frying pan was made to have a long shelf life, and in order to do that, it must withstand the abuse of other types of cookware. After all, we have been pitching this pan as the cream of the crop. How, can it stand up to that argument if it can be blemished by the sheer touch of a metal spatula?

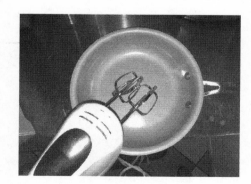

CHAPTER 6:

PRO TIPS YOU MAY NOT KNOW...
"ONES TO GROW ON!"

ALWAYS MARINATE YOUR MEATS BEFORE COOKING

You often think of marinating your steak or chicken breast during barbeque season. What if i told you that marinating your meat was actually good for your health? Well, it is. Marinating your beef, poultry and fish can help decrease the carcinogenic heterocyclic amines (hcas) that are produced when meat is grilled or cooked at high temperature levels. Marinating the meat first can reduced these levels by 99 percent, and if you add a touch of rosemary to the marinade that you make, it could help decrease this even more.

There are a few more reasons why using marinates can be beneficial to your meats prior to cooking. For instance, the acidic quality within the marinade can help slow down bacteria growth (when using citrus juices and vinegars.) But remember to always keep your meats soaking with your marinated in the fridge where your meats will stay cool and safe. Another great thing about marinates, besides the flavor, is that the juices can also tenderize the meat for you. This will help with digestion, so that the meat goes down smoothly. Lastly, marinates help keep the meat moist. So, you will never have to hear your mother-in-law tell you that your meat is dry and tough.
...and that's one to grow on!

COOKING WITH MEATS THAT HAVE FATS... IS THIS A SUBSTITUTE FOR OIL AND BUTTER?

Well...this is really a topic to talk about! If you are cooking with oils and butter, and also have fats on the meat that you are cooking with...you are just adding more oils to the cooking process. This will increase the fat content of your foods tremendously, and this is what you will be eating as a result of that! If there are recipes that call for oils or butter...check to see how much fat is on the meat. I know that you cannot calculate this precisely, but if you are aware that the meat you are cooking with has fat on it then you can scale back the amount of oil (or butter) that you are cooking with. This only makes sense because the recipe does not know how much fat is on your meat anyway. The fat content on meats will not only be a fat substitute, but it will also be something that flavors your foods in the process! If you cut down the amount of oil, grease and butter that you are cooking with you will be eating and serving much healthier recipes, keeping your cholesterol levels lower from not using that additional oil in your foods. **Now...that's one to grow on! :)**

KNOW YOUR FATS AND OILS: "COOKING AND CHOLESTEROL"

There is something to say about vegetable oils. They are the most "all-purpose oils" and probably the least expensive types of oils to cook with. There are oils that you may not have noticed or considered as an alternative to cook with, and here are just a few to keep in mind. Almond oil, coconut oil, grape seed oil and avocado oils, just to name a few for a little range of variation and diversity.

There are other oils that are great for foods but you may think about the heat exposure because these oils burn very easily when exposed to high cooking temperatures. These oils are normally utilized best when added to a salad or even a nice pasta dish or even best on vegetables for that added flavor! Such oils consist of oils that come from different types of nuts, sesame oil and we don't want to forget that extra virgin olive oil!

One oil that is extremely popular and not as expensive as the ones that were just mentioned is an "all favorite" the regular olive oil! This type of oil is a great cooking oil and adds a good flavor to your foods as well but just keep in mind again about the temperature that you are cooking with because this is one that can burn at high temperatures as well! Just read the labels to see which different flavors will go best with the foods you are cooking, and keep in mind the amount of heat that the oils can withstand…" and that's another one to grow on!"

GARNISHING WITH PARSLEY: IT'S MORE THAN JUST FOR DECORATION!

We are all familiar with the green leafed tree that decorates our plates at restaurants. Did you know that parsley was actually more than a garnish? This herb is a jack of all trades in the culinary world, and should be treated as such. First of all, the herb is packed with vitamin a, b, c, e, k, and it's great for your digestion. No wonder chefs have been putting it on your plate for years. It is supposed to be eaten after your meal. However, parsley can be used to eliminate waste, maintain gas, and relieves bloating, water retention and does this with its anti-inflammatory substances. This little green garnish can even help freshens your breath.

So, grab a leaf and bon a petite.

Parsley should be called the next Superfood. Not only is it packet with a ton of vitamins, but it can be used as an antibiotic and may aid against other bodily illnesses or infections as well. As an antibiotic, parsley boosts the immune system and may also help prevent other things like the common cold or flu, as well as treat bladder and urinary tract infections. The herb also contains high amounts of apigenin, which is an anticancer property. Eating parsley may help reduce the risk of beast, skin, prostrate and other cancers. The herb can also be used as an anti-inflammatory, as well as a detoxifier; eating it will definitely help keep you healthy. So, the next time a chef adorns your plate with a leaf of parsley, you should thank her for caring about your health enough to put it on your plate.

TEMPERATURE CHART OF GREATNESS!

What is it that make's a "master chef" so great at what they do? Well...that's a good question. But you better believe that they know their meat temperatures!!!

Frying Or In The Pan	Temperature	Cooking Time
Pancakes	350-400 Degrees	2-3 Minutes
Bacon	300-325 Degrees	8-10 Minutes
Canadian Bacon	275-300 Degrees	3-4 Minutes
Chicken	325-350 Degrees	25-40 Minutes
Eggs, Fried	250-275 Degrees	3-5 Minutes
Eggs, Scrambled	250-275 Degrees	3-5 Minutes
Fish	325-375 Degrees	5-10 Minutes
French Toast	300-325 Degrees	4-6 Minutes
Ham ½ Thick	325-350 Degrees	10-12 Minutes
Ham ¾ Thick	325-350 Degrees	14-16 Minutes
Hamburgers	325-375 Degrees	8-12 Minutes
Minute Steak	375-400 Degrees	4-5 Minutes
Pork Chops ½ Thick	325-375 Degrees	15-20 Minutes
Pork Chops ¾ Thick	325-375 Degrees	20-25 Minutes
Potatoes	300-350 Degrees	10-12 Minutes
Sausage, Link	300-325 Degrees	20-30 Minutes
Sausage, Precooked	325-350 Degrees	10-12 Minutes
Sandwiches, Grilled	300-325 Degrees	5-10 Minutes
Steak, Rare	350-400 Degrees	6-7 Minutes
Steak, Medium	350-400 Degrees	10-12 Minutes

CHAPTER 7:

USING THE CERAMIC TITANIUM'S PAN ACCESSORIES

The ceramic titanium pan isn't an ordinary pan. It comes with accessories that allow you to steam and deep fry food. This pan is so versatile you can use it for all of your cooking needs.

STEAMING YOUR WAY TO HEALTHIER FOOD

Steaming allows you to lock in loads of flavor, while cooking without any oil or fat. Steamed fish comes out moist and juicy. Steamed vegetables are perfectly cooked, and crisp. Simply place a couple cups of water in your red copper, and then the steaming tray. Heat the pain on high until the water boils. Place your desired food on the steaming tray, and cover the pan with the lid. Your food will be steamed perfectly in a few minutes.

DEEP FRIED DELICIOUSNESS

You can now enjoy delicious french fries and other fried favorites at home. Simply attach the deep frying basket to the side of your pan, and fill you pan with oil. Make sure you don't overfill your pan or the oil will pop up over the sides. Try using peanut oil because it has a high smoke point and neutral flavor. If you want to try something a little more exotic try using coconut or avocado oil.

CRISPIER FOOD WITHOUT ALL THE OIL

We all love fried food but sometimes we don't want all the unhealthiness. Oil adds a ton of calories and fat. The crisper tray allows you to enjoy all the crispiness of fried food without all of that oil. The crisper goes in your oven, and because there's space on the bottom cooks food evenly. Simply put your food in the crisper in a single layer and watch it cook. Nothing sticks to it so clean up is a breeze. The tray at the bottom keeps your oven clean. Enjoy a healthier version of all your favorites!

A LID YOU CAN COUNT ON

The ceramic titanium comes with a tempered glass lid. Tempered glass is strong enough to take on any challenge so you don't have to worry about breaking due to high heat. It also allows you to see your food as it cooks, so you never over cook anything. It has a small hole that lets out the right amount of steam so your pan never builds up to much pressure. You can cook confidently knowing that you have such a high quality accessory.

EVEN HEAT DISTRIBUTION FOR
PERFECTLY COOKED FOOD

The ceramic titanium has a stainless steel induction plate. This plate ensures that the heat from your stove is evenly distributed over the entire pan. This make sure that your food cooks evenly no matter where it is in the pan. You no longer have to worry about things in the middle cooking faster. You'll have perfectly cooked food everywhere.

THE HANDLE YOU'VE BEEN LOOKING FOR

This handle has you covered for all of your cooking needs. It's strongly constructed so that it can handle both high temperatures and the oven. It's riveted so that you never have to worry about it coming loose. It's been perfectly shaped so that it's easy for you to pick up and hold. Every detail has been thought of to make sure your cooking experience is as easy as possible.

CHAPTER 8:

LEARN HOW TO STORE FOODS PROPERLY!

Have you ever cleaned out your fridge and noticed all of the food that was sitting in your garbage can? Throwing food away can be very expensive and believe me, no one likes throwing money into the trash. This is one of the reasons why knowing the right ways to preserving your food is so important. This chapter will provide tips on how to store your food to avoid foodborne illnesses, preserve its shelf life and even save money.

STORE ALL LEFTOVERS IN AIRTIGHT, LEAK-PROOF CONTAINERS

Food safety is important when it comes to protecting our health. One of the best ways to do this is to store all of your leftovers from tonight's meal in air-tight, leak-proof containers. These containers protect against air-borne bacteria, pests and even leaks. When used correctly, they will protect the shelf life, taste and longevity of your leftovers. Now you and your family can continue to enjoy them for a little bit longer.

Glass containers with snap on lids are the best containers to use when storing food. Plastic containers can stain when storing food, such as spaghetti sauce or enchiladas. Glass containers do not stain as easily. Also, when storing food in plastic containers it is hard to see what is actually inside them. Storing food in glass containers help you see what is inside. Remember to label the date that you cooked and stored the food. This will give you a good idea of how old it is and when you need to dispose of it.

SEPARATE LEFTOVERS IN SMALL CONTAINERS TO COOL FASTER

There is a myth about storing hot or warm food in the fridge right away. Many people say that when you place large amounts of hot food into the fridge before cooling it down, it can cause the temperature to rise in the fridge, which can warm up all of the other food inside as well. So, the hot food will not only cool down rapidly, but it will warm up everything else. Even if this is the case, refrigerators were invented to keep food cool and not be affected by the warmth of newly cooked food. It is far more dangerous to let food sit out at room temperature to cool then to place it in the fridge while it is still warm.

When cooking large amounts of food, like stews, it can be easier to separate the leftovers into small containers. This can be beneficial for two reasons. First, it will allow the food to cool down much faster and at a safer temperature. Putting the food in more than one container lets it cool down without the risk of spoiling outside of the container or making the other food in the fridge warmer. Secondly, it becomes convenient for reheating small amounts for lunch or an individual dinner at home. Reheating the food in the microwave more than once can cause problems as well. So, this eliminates the problem of warming up more than you can eat at one time.

REFRIGERATE LEFTOVER FOODS WITHIN TWO HOURS OF COOKING AND COOLING

Refrigerating or freezing leftovers to preserve them is important. It is not only a healthy tip, but a financial one as well. In order to make sure that we and our families are eating healthy food, we need to make sure that we are preserving it correctly. Bacteria grows at a fast rate between the 40º f and 140º f range. Hot food must be kept at 140º f or higher to prevent bacteria. Food must be refrigerated at 41º f or lower to prevent everyone from getting sick.

Store your leftovers within two hours of cooking food and within one hour, if the temperature in the room is over 90 degrees. It is very important to adhere to these safety tips because it can be harmful to your health or that of your family if you don't. These tips can help keep you from getting sick from the bacteria that lingers around improperly handled food.

DIVIDE YOUR MEATS FOR A LONGER
AND SAFER SHELF LIFE

Just like fruits and vegetables, separating leftover meat is important to maintaining a longer shelf life. Cooling the meat and putting them in shallow or separate containers keeps it fresh longer. Divide the large portions into smaller quantities. If the food cooked in a very hot container then you want to put it into a container that doesn't keep it from cooling. One thing also to remember is not to pack the food tightly in the container or the refrigerator. Keeping a proper airflow helps maintain the temperature in the meat and helps it cool off. This way it will last longer and will be easy to grab when you want a good snack.

CHAPTER 9:

AMAZING UNIQUE RECIPES!

These recipes were made for anyone with any type of copper round pan, square pan, fry basket, steamer tray, crisper! When reading these recipes just remember that you are reading the views and opinions of the writer. We have also provided the nutritional values on all of these recipes "for all of you calorie counters out there." So...turn the page and "dive - head first" and get cooking! :)

BEEF:

Where's the beef you might ask, it's right here in this chapter! All the tasty, mouth watering, succulent, luscious, tender, rich, heavenly, divine, juicy and yummy beef recipes right here at your fingertips! Yes my friend's...beef is on the menu!

SHREDDED CABBAGE RICE ROLLS

Take a modern day twist on a classic. Cabbage rolls usually take a lot of preparation time with stuffing whole cabbage leaves. With this recipe you can save on time without compromising on the flavors that you love.

Prep time: 10 minutes
Cook time: 35 minutes
Servings: 4

Ingredients

1 1/2 lbs. Lean ground beef
1 small onion diced
1/2 shredded medium head of cabbage
1 can 14.5 oz stewed tomatoes
1 can 14.5 oz diced tomatoes
1 can tomato sauce

1 tsp. Sugar,
3 tsp. Cider vinegar
3/4 cup water
3/4 cup long-grain white rice
Sea salt
Pepper

Directions

➤ Cook ground beef for 5 minutes on high heat.
➤ Add the diced onions, cabbage, tomatoes, tomato sauce, sugar and vinegar with the ground beef and continue cooking for 4 minutes or until ground beef is browned.
➤ Add the water and rice to the skillet and simmer for 25 minutes, adding cheese, salt and pepper as desired.

Nutritional Facts:

Serving size 1 serving, calories 562, calories from fat 105, total fat 11.7g, Saturated fat 4.2g, cholesterol 152mg, sodium 1165mg, potassium 1891mg Carbohydrates 54.6g, dietary fiber 9.4g, sugars 17.3g, protein 59.8g

Very high in iron, high in phosphorus, high in selenium, very high in vitamin b6, very high in vitamin b12, very high in vitamin c, high in zinc

MINCED MEATBALL GARLIC SPAGHETTI

This recipe has all of the makings of a classic family recipe, but without all of the work. Here you can throw your uncooked noodles and cook them in the same spot as the sauce. So, pour yourself a glass of wine and enjoy this easy one pan spaghetti.

Prep time: 35 minutes
Cook time: 35 minutes
Servings: 4

Ingredients

24 oz pasta sauce (1 jar)
1 cup water
24 meatballs (fresh or precooked)
16 oz pasta, (broken in half)

1 cup mozzarella cheese (shredded part-skim)
½ cup parmesan cheese (grated)

Directions

> Pour the spaghetti sauce, meatballs and the noodles in to a non-stick pan until it boils.
> Cover the pan, and simmer for 25 minutes. Remember to stir the noodles to keep from sticking.
> When done, top with cheese and serve.

Nutritional Facts:

Serving size 903 g, amount per serving, calories 1,666, calories from fat 813, total fat 90.3g, saturated fat 35.6g, trans fat 0.0g, cholesterol 331mg, sodium 3562mg, potassium 741mg, total carbohydrates 123.5g, dietary fiber 10.4g, sugars 21.0g, protein 123.0g

I LOVE STEAK AND POTATOES SKILLET

Steak and potatoes in only 30 minutes. This recipe is paired with frozen potatoes and frozen veggies that give you a full balanced meal in under an hour.

Prep time: 30 minutes
Cook time: 30 minutes
Servings: 4

Ingredients

1 lb. Boneless beef sirloin steak, cut into 4 serving pieces
¾ tsp. Seasoned salt
½ tsp. Garlic-pepper blend

1 ½ cups frozen stir-fry vegetables
1 bag refrigerated home-style potato slices
4 oz or 1/2 cup shredded american-cheddar cheese blend

Directions -

> Place the steak into a non-stick pan and sprinkle with the seasoned salt and garlic pepper.
> Cook on medium heat for 2 minutes on each side.
> Remove steak from skillet and add vegetables, cooking for 2 minutes.
> Pour in potatoes and cook for 10 minutes.
> When done, pour in the steak and mix together before serving.

Nutritional Facts:

Serving size 407 g, amount per serving, calories 513
Calories from fat 150, total fat 16.7g, saturated fat 8.7g, cholesterol 131mg, sodium 554mg, potassium 1518mg, total carbohydrates 42.6g, dietary fiber 6.1g, sugars 2.9g
Protein 46.6g

Low in sugar, very high in iron, high in phosphorus, high in selenium, very high in vitamin b6, very high in vitamin b12, high in vitamin c, high in zinc

NEW DELI INDIAN CURRY SKILLET

Description
Indian meets chinese. This dish will have you adding ground beef to a curry and then throwing it over rice. What it won't have you do is dislike the flavor.

Prep time: 50 minutes
Cook time: 50 minutes
Servings: 6

Ingredients
1 ½ cups uncooked white rice
1 lb. Lean ground beef
1 small chopped onion, chopped (1/4 cup)
1 chopped clove garlic
2 tsp. Gingerroot (grated)
1 tsp. Tomato paste

1 tsp. Salt
2 tsp. Ground cumin
2 tsp. Chili powder
1 tsp. Garam masala
29 oz diced tomatoes (2 cans)
3 tsp. Chopped fresh cilantro

Directions -
> Pour beef, onion, garlic and gingerroot into non-stick pan and cook for 7 minutes.
> Add the rest of the ingredients and simmer uncovered for 10 minutes.
> Pour over the cooked rice, add cilantro and serve.

Nutritional Facts:
Serving size 276 g, amount per serving, calories 348, calories from fat 51, total fat 5.7g, saturated fat 2.0g, cholesterol 68mg, sodium 459mg19%, potassium 749mg
Total carbohydrates 45.0g, dietary fiber 3.0g, sugars 4.4g, protein 27.9g,

Very high in iron, high in selenium, very high in vitamin b6, very high in vitamin b12, high in zinc

NO MAS TORTILLA BURRITOS

One of my favorite and, most fun to make! If you're ever in doubt...burritos are on the menu! A nice big chunk of "mouth watering mexican flavored bliss" is about to happen for dinner. Dive in and taste this mexican goodness!

Description

Want all the taste of a burrito but don't want the carbs. This one stop no tortilla ground beef burritos has all of the makings of a great dish, but throw out the tortilla. You won't even miss it.

Prep time: 30 minutes
Cook time: 30 minutes
Servings: 4

Ingredients

1 lb. Lean ground beef
1 pkg. Taco seasoning mix
16 oz can red kidney beans
1 cup thick & chunky salsa

1 cup water
1 cup mexican style shredded four cheese
1/3 cup sour cream
1 large chopped green onion

Directions

> Add all ingredients to a non-stick skillet and bring to a boil for 5 minutes.
> When cooled off, add sour cream, onions and serve.

Nutritional Facts:

Serving size 414 g, amount per serving, calories 511, calories from fat 193, total fat 21.5g, saturated fat 11.3g, trans fat 0.0g, cholesterol 139mg, sodium 1491mg, potassium 998mg, total carbohydrates 28.6g, dietary fiber 6.4g, sugars 2.6g, protein 48.7g

Low in sugar, very high in iron. High in phosphorus, high in selenium, very high in vitamin b6, very high in vitamin b12 high in zinc

SIZZLING SOUTHWEST SHERRY FILET MIGNON

Who doesn't love steak and onions? Top with sweet sherry and a toasted french baguette and you will have a meal that will make your mouth water for more. – just wrote this one. Was not on the original.

Prep time: 45 minutes
Cook time: 45 minutes
Servings: 4

Ingredients

1 lb. Filet mignon (trimmed and cut into 4 steaks)
1/2 tsp. Minced dried onion
1/2 tsp. Salt
1/2 tsp. Freshly ground pepper
2 large chopped sweet onions

1/3 cup dry sherry wine
1 tsp. All-purpose flour
1 cup beef broth
2 tsp. Fresh chopped thyme
4 slices baguettes (toasted whole-grain)
1/2 cup shredded swiss cheese

Directions

> Season the steaks with onion, salt and pepper and add them to a non-stick skillet.
> Cook for 3 minutes on each side.
> Remove the steaks and add the add the onions and sherry to the skillet.
> Cover and cook on high for 8 minutes
> Pour the flour, broth, thyme and bring to a small boil.
> Add the steaks back to the skillet and top with a slice of baguette and cheese
> Place in the oven and cook for 2 minutes.

Nutritional Facts:

Serving size 316 g, amount per serving, calories 407, calories from fat 111,, total fat 12.3g, saturated fat 5.5g, cholesterol 87mg, sodium 787mg33%, potassium 659mg, total carbohydrates 27.6g, dietary fiber 2.7g, sugars 4.5g, protein 41.4g

High in niacin, high in phosphorus, very high in selenium, high in vitamin b6, high in zinc

GARLIC AND MUSHROOM GROUND BEEF STROGANOF

My mother used to make this dish with pieces of stew meat and would place it over rice. Here is a nice take on the dish with your own flare. Share your mom that you can share her up in the kitchen and do it in style.

Prep time: 20 minutes
Cook time: 35 minutes
Servings: 4

Ingredients

1 lb. Ground beef
1 chopped onion
1 tsp. Garlic powder
1/4 tsp. Black pepper

1/2 pound chopped fresh mushrooms
1 can condensed cream of mushroom soup
1 1/2 cups sour cream
1/2 pound cooked egg noodles

Directions -

> -add the onion and ground beef into a non-stick skillet and cook until meat is brown.
> - pour in garlic powder, and mushrooms. Cook for 3 minutes.
> - pour in the soup and simmer for 10 minutes.
> - serve over rice or noodles and add sour cream to the mixture.

Nutritional Facts:

Serving size 418 g, amount per serving, calories 564, calories from fat 279, total fat 31.0g48%, saturated fat 15.2g76%, trans fat 0.0g, cholesterol 156mg52%, sodium 620mg26%, potassium 880mg25%, total carbohydrates 28.1g9%, dietary fiber 1.9g8%, sugars 3.8g, protein 43.1g

Low in sugar, very high in iron, high in selenium, very high in vitamin b6, very high in vitamin b12

BIG TEXAS BEAN AND BACON BURGERS

Cooked in a skillet and not over the bbq. This kicking bacon burger dish still packs a punch and is very easy to make.

Prep time: 5 minutes
Cook time: 15 minutes
Servings: 6

Ingredients
1 1/2 lbs. Ground beef
1 can condensed bean with bacon soup
1/2 cup water

1 tsp. Horseradish
6 slices yellow cheddar cheese
6 sesame topped hamburger buns

Directions -
> Create 6 burgers from the ground beef.
> Add the burgers in a non-stick pan and cook for 10 minutes.
> Pour in the soup, water and horseradish and bring to a boil.
> Cover and cook for 5 minutes.
> Add the cheese and cook until melted.
> Serve on the buns.

Nutritional Facts:
Serving size 210 g, amount per serving, calories 422, calories from fat 151, total fat 16.8g, saturated fat 7.6g, trans fat 0.0g, cholesterol 127mg, sodium 667mg, potassium 608mg, total carbohydrates 21.1g, dietary fiber 1.1g, sugars 4.6g, protein 44.1g

Very high in iron, high in phosphorus, high in selenium, very high in vitamin b6, very high in vitamin b12, high in zinc

TENDER TERIYAKI BRAISED BEEF & BROCCOLI

Nothing is simpler than cooking everything in the same pot, and an added bonus is when it doesn't take a long time. Rice, vegetables, and beef make this entrée an entire meal in one, and the teriyaki sauce provides a flavorful theme to the dish. Just toss in, stir, and dinner will be ready in no time!

Prep time: 10 minutes
Cook time: 15 minutes
Servings: 5

Ingredients

1 lb. Lean ground beef (at least 80%)
12 oz frozen chopped broccoli (1 bag)
1/2 cup chopped green onions (1 bunch - separate white and green parts)

1/2 cup of chopped shallots
3 cups cold cooked white rice
1 cup marinade (thick teriyaki sauce)

Directions

> In a 5-quart pot, cook beef over medium-high heat, stirring frequently, until brown adding with salt to taste...keep the juice.
> Also cook broccoli as directed.
> Stir in green onions and shallots to pan with beef, and cook for about a minute or so.
> Add rice, teriyaki sauce. Stir as it cooks, just for a couple of minutes...till rice is cooked.
> Last add broccoli and green onions...stir for about 30 seconds. Done!

Nutritional Facts:

Serving size 344 g, amount per serving, calories 676, calories from fat 89, total fat 9.9g, saturated fat 2.4g, trans fat 0.0g, cholesterol 81mg, sodium 1281mg, potassium 774mg, total carbohydrates 106.6g, dietary fiber 4.0g, sugars 7.7g, protein 37.7g

Low in saturated fat, high in iron, high in selenium, very high in vitamin b6, very high in vitamin b12, high in vitamin c

JUICY MARINATED DIJON QUARTER LOIN

Flank steak is a great and versatile meat to marinade, especially if the sauce is extraordinarily tasty. You can't go wrong with red wine vinegar, dijon mustard, and lemon in anything, but imagine all mixed together with worcestershire sauce, garlic, & black pepper! Marinade. 6 hours, and get ready to wipe the water from your mouth afterwards.

Prep time: 15 minutes
Cook time: 10 minutes
Servings: 4

Ingredients

1/2 cup vegetable oil
1/4 cup red wine vinegar
2 tablespoons fresh lemon juice
2 tablespoons worcestershire sauce
1 tablespoon dijon mustard

2 cloves garlic, minced
1/2 teaspoon ground black pepper
1/2 teaspoon onion powder
1/2 teaspoon sea salt
1 1/2 pounds flank steak

Directions

> In a medium sized container, mix the vinegar with the oil. Add lemon juice, worcestershire sauce, mustard, garlic, onion powder, salt and ground black pepper. Place meat in dish and soak the steak with the marinade by pouring it all over, coating generously. Cover...put in refrigerate for 5-6 hours.

> Turn on the griddle for medium-high heat and add oil. Add steaks to the griddle. (you are done with the marinade.) Cook meat on the grill. About 6 minutes per side or to your liking.

Nutritional Facts:

Serving size 234 g, amount per serving, calories 590, calories from fat 375, total fat 41.6g, saturated fat 11.3g, trans fat 0.0g, cholesterol 94mg, sodium 459mg, potassium 613mg, total carbohydrates 2.9g, sugars 1.9g, protein 47.7g
Low in sugar. High in niacin, high in selenium

SUCCULENT PAN-SEARED GARLIC TENDERLOIN

There are not many more basic main courses than a juicy piece of steak. The great thing about straightforward meals is that they are fast, and with the right piece of meat, they are delicious. We will keep it simple: steak, salt, and pepper. If it ain't broke, don't fix it as the saying goes!

Prep time: 15 minutes
Cook time: 15 minutes
Servings: 2

Ingredients

12 oz steaks (can use 2 6oz flat iron tenderloin)
1 tbsp. Olive oil
1/2 teaspoon garlic powder

1/2 teaspoon onion powder
1/2 teaspoon black pepper
1 pinch of salt (to taste)

Directions

›   After bringing steak to room temperature, pat the meat with a paper towel to remove moisture. Season with the salt and pepper and onion and garlic powders.
›   Add oil to your pan while heating pan.
›   Let the steaks cook for a few minutes turning them over and repeating after first side is cooked, then flip and cook for another 3 minutes. Turn over the steaks and cook for another 2 to 3 minutes. Check steaks to see if they are cooked to your liking, but each side should be at least a golden brown.
›   Slice and serve the steak after letting it cool for several minutes.

Nutritional Facts:

Serving size 180 g, amount per serving, calories 404, calories from fat 140, total fat 15.5g, saturated fat 3.9g, cholesterol 153mg, sodium 155mg, potassium 588mg, total carbohydrates 1.3g, protein 61.7g

Low in sodium, very low in sugar, very high in selenium, high in vitamin b12, high in zinc

THICK STACKED SIZZLING BURGERS ON THE STOVETOP

Burgers: american as apple pie, which should remind you not to forget dessert. However, many grill their burgers without realizing they can quickly be cooked on the stovetop using a griddle or skillet. With the right meat and the proper technique, the family can have burgers year round, but try not to get addicted!

Prep time: 10 minutes
Cook time: 10 minutes (or less)
Servings: 6

Ingredients

1 1/2 pounds ground beef, 80% to 85% lean
9.5 oz hamburger buns (6 buns)
1/4 stick butter (use oil as substitute if desired)
Pinch salt
Pinch fresh black pepper
6 slices cheese

Burger toppings:
2 sliced tomatoes,
1/4 onion (sliced)
2 pickles
3 tbsp. Ketchup
2 tbsp. Mustard
6 lettuce leaves

Directions

> Shape the ground beef into 6 big and chunky patties.
> Melt butter on a pan over medium heat.
> Lightly butter the buns, then toasting them to your desired liking. Move the buns to a clean plate.
> Using the same pan, cook the patties for several minutes. Add a pinch of salt and pepper to each and continue to cook for 3 to 4 minutes.
> Flip the burgers and repeat the process, adding a little more salt and pepper than before. Cook for another several minutes or until cooked to your desired liking.

Nutritional Facts:

serving size 412 g, amount per serving, calories 779, calories from fat 315, total fat 35.0g, saturated fat 17.3g, cholesterol 211mg, sodium 1297mg, potassium 1047mg, total carbohydrates 42.6g, dietary fiber 3.6g, sugars 9.7g, protein 70.9g

Very high in iron, high in selenium, very high in vitamin b6, very high in vitamin b12, high in zinc

POULTRY:

In this section...chicken is on the menu! When preparing these gourmet poultry pounders...your friends will think you went to culinary school for years or married a professional chef for all the wrong reasons. All of these authentic menu item will have you running to the hen house to re-stock your refrigerator with these mouth watering marinated delicacies! This section will be the best thing that has happened to you in a long time...all you have to do is pick a chick!

ZESTY BASIL CRUSTED CHICKEN

This low in calories and carbohydrates chicken and vegetables dish is not only easy to cook but it is really tasty. You won't believe that it's good for you because of its amazing, mouthwatering, lip-smacking taste.

Prep time: 5 minutes
Cook time: 35 minutes
Servings: 3

Ingredients

Salt and pepper for taste
1 pound boneless, skinless chicken meat, cut into bite-sized pieces
1 red bell pepper, washed and diced
8 ounces mushrooms, cleaned and sliced

2 cups zucchini or other summer squash (washed, stemmed and sliced)
3 garlic cloves (minced or pressed)
8 ounces fresh basil (chopped)

Directions

> Season the chicken with salt and pepper for taste.
> Add the chicken to a non-stick skillet, cooking on both sides until brown.
> Pour in the rest of the ingredients and cook for 3 minutes.
> Serve

Nutritional Facts:

Serving size 420 g, amount per serving, calories 350calories from fat 110, total fat 12.2g Saturated fat 3.1g, cholesterol 135mg, sodium 147mg, potassium 1124mg, total carbohydrates 10.4g, dietary fiber 3.7g15%, sugars 4.5g, protein 50.0g

Low in sodium, high in iron, high in manganese, very high in niacin, high in phosphorus, high in riboflavin, high in selenium, very high in vitamin a, very high in vitamin b6, very high in vitamin c

GRILLED COWBOY CORNBREAD CHICKEN

Chicken and cornbread is a staple in any american household and is something that you can never get enough of. This recipe will bring you back to the western days and you will love the taste of bbq chicken cooked right into the buttery cornbread.

Prep time: 5 minutes
Cook time: 45 minutes
Servings: 6

Ingredients

8.5 oz corn muffin mix (1 box)
½ cup sour cream
2 tbsp. Butter, melted
1 egg
½ cups corn kernels
1 diced red onion
Kosher salt

Freshly ground black pepper
2 cups shredded chicken (rotisserie best)
1 1/3 cup bbq sauce
1 oz lime juice
1 cup shredded cheddar
8oz gouda cheese (shredded)
¼ cup diced scallions

Directions

> Bake the corn muffin mix, sour cream, butter, egg and corn in a non-stick pan for 20 minutes on 400 degrees.
> In another non-stick pan cook onions and chicken until chicken is fully cooked.
> Add the bbq sauce and the lime juice and continue cooking.
> After cornbread has cooled, poke holes and pour in the bbq sauce, chicken and cheddar cheese.
> Bake for another 20 minutes. Serve with scallions.

Nutritional Facts:

Serving size 270 g, amount per serving, calories 577, calories from fat 239, total fat 26.5g, saturated fat 15.1g, trans fat 0.0g, cholesterol 134mg, sodium 1494mg, potassium 373mg, total carbohydrates 54.2g, dietary fiber 1.7g, sugars 23.9g, protein 31.7g

SIZZLING SOUTHWESTERN CHEDDAR CHICKEN–

This is a sizzling chicken recipe that has a little kick. Where is a tortilla when you need one? You can use it to sop up the leftover salsa or cool down your mouth before the next bite. – wrote this one. Was not included in the original.

Prep time: 5 minutes
Cook time: 25 minutes
Servings: 4

Ingredients

1 lb. Boneless skinless chicken breasts
4oz taco seasoning
1 tsp. Cayenne pepper
Kosher salt
2 cloves minced garlic

1 chopped small red onion
2 chopped red bell peppers
15-oz. Can black beans (drained)
2 cups shredded cheddar
1/2 cup chopped fresh cilantro

Directions

> Sprinkle the chicken with the taco seasoning, cayenne pepper and salt.
> Add it to the non-stick skillet and cook for 6 minutes on each side. Take chicken out when done.
> Next, add the rest of the ingredients and cook for 7 minutes.
> Re-add chicken to the skillet and cook for 2 minutes with cheese mixture.
> Garnish and serve.

Nutritional Facts:

Serving size 386 g, amount per serving, calories 502, calories from fat 148, total fat 16.5g, saturated fat 6.7g, trans fat 0.0g, cholesterol 122mg, sodium 1012mg, potassium 961mg, total carbohydrates 30.4g, dietary fiber 6.8g, sugars 4.4g, protein 56.7g

Low in sugar, high in niacin, high in phosphorus, high in selenium, very high in vitamin c

FIESTA CHICKEN

Fiesta chicken with salsa and peppers is a great way to liven up a normal everyday meal. The peppers and salsa will spice up this dish and will be a great hit with the family. Pair with a margarita or a corona to make for a fun night.

Prep time: 5 minutes
Cook time: 30 minutes
Servings: 4

Ingredients

1 ¼ cup chicken broth
5oz couscous (box of roasted garlic-and-olive-oil)
2 tsp. Vegetable oil
1lb chicken thighs (6 large bone/skin-on)
1 ½ tsp. Kosher salt
¾ tsp. Ground pepper
3 medium bell peppers (colorful)
½ medium onion

2 cloves garlic

(salsa verde ingredients mix below)
¼ cup fresh parsley
¼ cup fresh basil
1 green onion
¼ cup extra-virgin olive oil
2 tbsp. Capers
1 ½ tbsp. Fresh lemon juice

Directions

> Boil the chicken broth and add to the couscous. Set aside.
> Place chicken in a non-stick skillet, sprinkle with salt and pepper and cook for 7 minutes on each side.
> Transfer to a plate and add cook peppers for 4 minutes.
> Add the chicken on top of the peppers and bake in the oven on 400 degrees for 10 minutes.
> Pour the chicken, onions, capers and lemon juice on top of the couscous and serve.

Nutritional Facts:

Serving size 366 g, amount per serving, calories 530calories from fat 219, total fat 24.4g, saturated fat 4.8g, cholesterol 101mg, sodium 1348mg, potassium 663mg, total carbohydrates 36.0g, dietary fiber 4.5g, sugars 4.8g, protein 40.4g

High in niacin, high in vitamin a, very high in vitamin c

SONOMA MUSHROOM AND WINE CHICKEN

Ever dream of cooking in a french kitchen? This easy french chicken will make you feel like you are cooking in one of the top culinary schools in paris, and with ease. So, take out a pan and spatula, and give it a try.

Prep time: 5 minutes
Cook time: 20 minutes
Servings: 4

Ingredients

1/2 lb. Chicken (3 large cutlets sliced)
Sea salt
Ground pepper
½ cup all-purpose flour
1 medium sliced sweet onion
½ lb. Sliced mushrooms

1 sliced yellow bell pepper
1 oz tomato paste (about 2 tsps)
½ cup white wine
½ cup beef broth
14.5 oz chopped tomatoes (1 can)
½ tsp. Butter

Directions

➤ Rub salt, pepper and flour onto the chicken.
➤ Place the chicken into a non-stick skillet and cook on both sides for 3 minutes.
➤ Transfer the chicken onto a plate.
➤ Cook the mushrooms, onions, tomato paste and peppers in the skillet for 7 minutes.
➤ Add the wine, broth and tomatoes, and cook for 4 minutes.
➤ Re-add the chicken and butter when it starts to boil and cook for another 4 minutes
➤ Serve.

Nutritional Facts:

Serving size 356 g, amount per serving, calories 233, calories from fat 27
Total fat 3.0g, saturated fat 0.9g, cholesterol 45mg, sodium 193mg, potassium 777mg, total carbohydrates 24.4g, dietary fiber 3.7g, sugars 7.3g, protein 22.3g
Low in saturated fat, high in niacin, high in selenium, high in vitamin a, very high in vitamin b6, very high in vitamin c

SIMPLY ITALIAN MUSHROOM CHICKEN RAVIOLI

Italian chicken ravioli is a fast, easy recipe that is bursting with flavor. The mushrooms, tomatoes, garlic and cheese brings you all of the flavor that we have grown accustomed to with italian food, but without all of the hassle in the kitchen.

Prep time: 15 minutes
Cook time: 15 minutes
Servings: 4

Ingredients

Kosher salt
9-ounce package of cheese ravioli
1 tbsp. Olive oil for drizzling
1 ¼ lbs. Boneless, skinless chicken breast cut into chunks
Fresh ground pepper
8 ounces of sliced white mushrooms

1 cup of diced cherry tomatoes
2 cloves of sliced garlic
2 tsp. Red wine vinegar
1/3 cup of chicken broth
2 tsp. Grated parmesan cheese
¼ cup fresh parsley

Directions

> Cook ravioli.
> In a non-stick skillet cook the chicken for two minutes on both sides.
> Transfer to a plate.
> Add the mushrooms and tomatoes and cook for 7 minutes.
> Return the chicken, ravioli, chicken broth and parmesan cheese and cook for 5 minutes.
> Garnish and serve.

Nutritional Facts:

Serving size 353 g, amount per serving, calories 534, calories from fat 148, total fat 16.5g, saturated fat 4.7g, trans fat 0.0g, cholesterol 183mg, sodium 442mg, potassium 808mg, total carbohydrates 35.9g, dietary fiber 1.3g, sugars 2.3g, protein 60.6g
Low in sugar, very high in niacin, high in phosphorus, high in selenium, very high in vitamin b6, high in vitamin b12

CREAMY THICK AND HEARTY SHEPHERD'S PI

The smell of sweet, buttery mashed potatoes blanketing the heaps of chicken and vegetables stirs the hunger within our stomachs. Who said that shepherd's pie only had to be made with beef? Try this recipe and you will be thankful that you made the switch.

Prep time: 15 minutes
Cook time: 15 minutes
Servings: 4

Ingredients

2 cups cooked chicken cut into cubes
1 (16-ounce) package frozen mixed vegetables
10.5 oz cream of mushroom soup (1 can condensed can)

1/2 cup milk
1/4 tsp. Onion powder
1/4 tsp. Black pepper
4 cups mashed potatoes (hot)

Directions -

> In a non-stick skillet pour in all ingredients that are listed above, with the exception of the potatoes. Make sure you stir all of these ingredients after you pour them in.
> Cook for 7-8 minutes, remember to stir often. (sauce will thicken while heating)
> Serve over potatoes.

Nutritional Facts:
Serving size 531 g, amount per serving, calories 428, calories from fat 72, total fat 8.0g, saturated fat 2.7g, cholesterol 61mg, sodium 885mg, potassium 1078mg, total carbohydrates 58.1g, dietary fiber 5.0g, sugars 5.5g, protein 30.8g
Vitamin a 100%

High in niacin. Very high in vitamin a, high in vitamin b6

TURKEY SMOKED ITALIAN SAUSAGE
GARLIC & BASIL PASTA

Italian sausage made with turkey? This is an abomination. Try this recipe and you will learn to love the flavor and the low calorie count.

Prep time: 15 minutes
Cook time: 15 minutes
Servings: 6

Ingredients
1 lb. Turkey sausage (1 package sliced)
1/2 cup chopped green bell pepper
14.5 oz diced tomatoes (1 can with basil, garlic & oregano)
1 cup tomato sauce

1-1/2 cups water
8 oz dry uncooked rigatoni pasta
1oz grated parmesan cheese
1oz parsley (garnish)

Directions -
> In a non-stick skillet add the turkey sausage and brown it...cooking for 5 about minutes turning occasionally.
> Add the chopped green peppers to the skillet and cook for 2 more minutes sprinkling a pinch of salt and pepper for flavor.
> Next, combine the water, tomatoes sauce and pasta...bringing it all to a boil.
> Simmer the dish turning the head down and covered for 15 minutes.
> Take the grated parmesan cheese and shower the meal adding the parsley for garnish.

Nutritional Facts:
Serving size 279 g, amount per serving, calories 407, calories from fat 212, total fat 23.6g, saturated fat 7.7g, trans fat 0.2g, cholesterol 94mg, sodium 841mg, potassium 630mg, total carbohydrates 26.5g, dietary fiber 1.7g, sugars 3.9g, protein 21.9g
High in vitamin c

FLAVORED GARLIC PARMESAN TURKEY & BROCCOLI PASTA

Turkey is an overlooked meat if thanksgiving is not on the mind, especially when a quick dinner is desired. However, it can be a perfect substitute for any of the more thought-about proteins! This particular entrée pairs the turkey with broccoli and pasta, and with a few spices it will easily convince you that chicken is not the only bird available on weeknights.

Prep time: 15 minutes
Cook time: 20 minutes
Servings: 4

Ingredients
¾ pound orecchiette
2 cups broccoli florets
3 tablespoons olive oil
1 pound ground turkey
2 cloves garlic, chopped
1/4 cup chopped onion

1 teaspoon fennel seed
½ teaspoon crushed red pepper
Kosher salt
1/2 cup shredded parmesan + more for serving

Directions
> Cook the pasta as directed on the box instructions, and during the final minute of the pasta cooking, add the broccoli. Make sure you drain the water out of the pot.
> Return all then return to pot.
> While the pasta a broccoli is cooking, add 1 tablespoon of the oil to your skillet and heat. After the oil is warm, place the rest of the ingredients in the skillet and cook. Make sure you cook for several minutes or until the meat is done, mixing the ingredients while cooking. Add salt as desired.
> Pour the turkey and other ingredients into the pot and mix with the pasta, the other two tablespoons of oil, and broccoli. You may sprinkle the dish with parmesan cheese before serving.

Nutritional Facts:

Serving size 279 g, amount per serving, calories 706, calories from fat 265, total fat 29.4g, saturated fat 6.6g, trans fat 0.0g, cholesterol 131mg, sodium 264mg, potassium 494mg, total carbohydrates 70.7g, dietary fiber 4.6g, sugars 4.2g, protein 45.1g

Low in sodium, low in sugar, high in selenium

CREAMY & CHEESY TURKEY ALFREDO WITH SPINACH

Chicken alfredo is an essential entrée, but a different bird can liven up the party from time to time. Ground turkey is an excellent change to the dish, but make sure not to ignore the chicken every time! The italian seasoning keeps the meal true to form, and the spinach and tomatoes add a fresh taste to the creamy classic, making it enjoyable for new and old fans alike.

Prep time: 10 minutes
Cook time: 15 minutes
Servings: 4

Ingredients

2 cups rotini pasta (6 oz)
1 lb. Lean ground turkey
1 teaspoon italian seasoning
1/4 teaspoon salt
1/2 crushed red pepper
3 cups firmly packed fresh spinach leaves

1 container (10 oz) refrigerated reduced-fat alfredo pasta sauce
1 can (14.5 oz) petite diced tomatoes, un-drained
1/4 cup shredded parmesan cheese (1 oz)

Directions

›   Using the package directions, cook the pasta to desired liking and drain.
›   While the pasta is cooking, cook turkey, italian seasoning, crushed red pepper, and salt in a nonstick skillet over medium-high heat for approximately 5-7 minutes while stirring. Drain when ready.
›   Mix the spinach and turkey together. Leave the pan uncovered and let cook for 2-3 minutes while stirring occasionally, the stir in pasta sauce and tomatoes when you see the spinach is cooked down. Continue to stir for just a few minutes and then finally add the pasta.
›   Add cheese, cover, melting the cheese cooking for about 3-5 min on low.

Nutritional Facts:

Serving size 361 g, amount per serving, calories 634, calories from fat 225, total fat 25.0g, saturated fat 12.1g, trans fat 0.0g, cholesterol 146mg, sodium 3761mg, potassium 836mg, total carbohydrates 62.2g, dietary fiber 1.9g, sugars 3.0g, protein 40.9g

Low in sugar

THE FRESHEST, EASIEST GARLIC CHICKEN IN THE COOP

Quick and simple: two great words to hear regarding entrees. This chicken dish uses the most basic of ingredients, and provides mouth-watering taste. Luckily for any cook, the elements to this entrée may already be in the kitchen, which makes this meal perfect if time is an issue and a hungry family waits.

Prep time: 12 minutes
Cook time: 15-25 minutes
Servings: 4 servings

Ingredients

1 1/2 lbs. Chicken breasts (boneless and skinless)
4 garlic cloves, minced
1/4 cup chopped onions
1/4 teaspoon lemon juice

4 tablespoons of brown sugar
1 tablespoon of olive oil
1 tablespoon of salt
1 tablespoon of ground pepper
*add spices as desired

Directions

> Turn the oven on to 450°f to get nice and warm.
> Sauté garlic and onions with lemon juice and olive oil in a small nonstick pan.
> Take the pan off of the heat and add the brown sugar.
> Use salt and pepper to season the chicken to your liking.
> Coat chicken with garlic and brown sugar mixture. Place the breasts in the oven.
> Bake the dish for 20-25 minutes. Make sure to keep checking the chicken because the cooking time may vary on the size of your chicken breasts use a knife to cut into the chicken to make sure not to dry it out.

Nutritional Facts:

Serving size 199 g, amount per serving, calories 399, calories from fat 146, total fat 16.2g, saturated fat 4.0g, cholesterol 151mg, sodium 1894mg, potassium 469mg, total carbohydrates 11.5g, dietary fiber 0.6g, sugars 9.1g, protein 49.7g
High in niacin, high in selenium, high in vitamin b6

MEATLOVER'S ROASTED CHICKEN WITH SAUTEED PROSCIUTTO

This entrée is a light and fresh mixture of meat and vegetables. Using basic ingredients, the dish provides tastes everyone can recognize and enjoy. The chicken and zucchini complement each other well and the prosciutto adds a salty, flavorful presence to the main course. The citrus from the lemon gives a perfect end to a dish that spans many flavors, but in little time!

Prep time: 15 minutes
Cook time: 15 minutes
Servings: 4

Ingredients

2 lbs. Chicken breasts (about 4 boneless and skinless)
1/2 teaspoon kosher salt
1/2 teaspoon black pepper
2 tablespoons olive oil
1/4 pound (about 8 slices) prosciutto

2 small zucchini, thinly sliced into half-moons
1 small yellow squash
1 red pepper, sliced
1 clove garlic, thinly sliced
2 oz lemon (zest and juice)

Directions

›   Turn the oven on to 425º to be ready for baking the chicken.
›   Use the lemon zest and a pinch each of salt and pepper to season the chicken.
›   In your skillet, heat 1 tablespoon of the oil over medium-high heat, heat the chicken up till it starts to look done. Probably cooking for about a couple of minutes on each side.
›   Afterwards, put the chicken in the oven and bake it for approximately 7-10 minutes.
›   During this time, add the remaining oil in another pan. Cook the prosciutto on medium for just a couple of minutes on each side, then place on a clean plate. You know its done when it starts to get crispy.
›   Mix in and cook the zucchini, squash, red pepper, garlic cooking for 3 minutes in the skillet. Make sure you add salt and pepper to add flavor.

> When done, add everything to the chicken. Take the lemon and shower the lemon juice all over the dish and serve.

Nutritional Facts:

Serving size 397 g, amount per serving, calories 561, calories from fat 231, total fat 25.7g Saturated fat 6.2g, cholesterol 217mg, sodium 837mg, potassium 953mg, total carbohydrates 6.9g, dietary fiber 2.1g, sugars 3.1g, protein 73.1g

Low in sugar, high in niacin, high in selenium, high in vitamin b6, high in vitamin c

FISH:

Try any one of these light, flakey and delicious calorie counting entrees that will make float your boat. This is a great way to learn techniques that will perk up your plate and give you the healthy meal that your tummy is craving and deserves! So...turn a few of the pages, even with your eyes closed, and just pick-a-dish! You will be satisfied with any choice in this section! And after you've tried a few...you'll know that we've casted our lines and "reeled you in!"

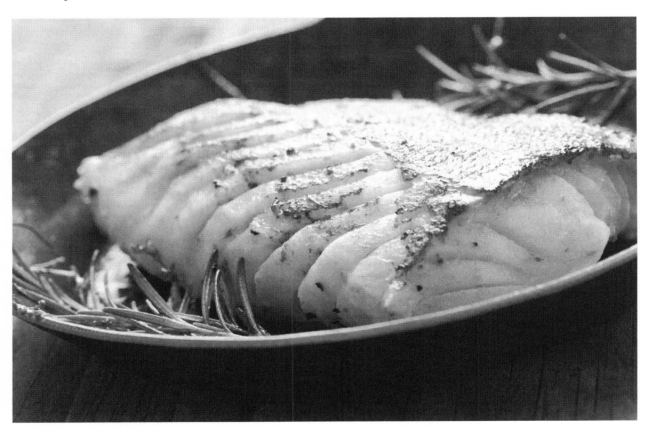

PAN-FRIED BAYOU GARLIC CATFISH

Catfish is a southern staple and a delightful entrée for many occasions. Despite the norm, there is no need for a deep fryer when it comes to this blackened course; the spices will exercise your senses fine on their own and in a more healthy fashion. Quick, easy, delicious, and without the mess of batter; what else could you ask for?

Prep time: 15 minutes
Cook time: 10 minutes
Servings: 6

Ingredients

1.5 tablespoons paprika
1/2 tablespoon cayenne pepper
2.5 teaspoons salt
2 teaspoons lemon pepper
1.5 teaspoons garlic powder
1 teaspoons ground pepper

1/2 teaspoon red pepper
1.5 teaspoons dried basil
1 teaspoon onion powder
1 teaspoon thyme
6 catfish fillets
1 cup unsalted butter, melted

Directions

> Place a pan or skillet over medium high heat.
> Stir all the spices together in a mixing container.
> Melt butter. Dip the catfish to use it as a base in order to coat both sides of fish with a little bit of the spice mixture for each fillet. After seasoning, let the rest on wax paper.
> After placing fish in hot pan, divide & drizzle remaining melted butter over each filet.
> Cook the fish until desired liking or when starting to brown or flaky just a few minutes on each side. Serve hot. Mmmmmmm...delicious.

Nutritional Facts:

Serving size 205 g, amount per serving, calories 501, calories from fat 389, total fat 43.2g
Saturated fat 21.7g, cholesterol 157mg, sodium 1273mg, potassium 600mg, total
carbohydrates 2.9g, dietary fiber 1.2g, sugars 0.6g, protein 25.8g
Very low in sugar, high in vitamin b12

SAVORY BASIL SHRIMP AND CHEESY GNOCCHI

Shrimp is a superfood, and italians know their way around a kitchen; it's time for you to experience the best of both, and all you will need is a skillet! The most difficult part of this meal is finding good gnocchi, but it shouldn't be too hard to come across. After your shopping is done, mix the shrimp, gnocchi, vegetables, and classic herbs and spices and you have a full course meal ready to serve in one dish.

Prep time: 15 minutes
Cook time: 15 minutes
Servings: 4

Ingredients

1 tablespoon plus 2 teaspoons extra-virgin olive oil, divided
1 16-ounce package shelf-stable gnocchi
1/2 cup sliced shallots
1 bunch asparagus (about 1 pound), trimmed and cut into thirds
3/4 cup reduced-sodium chicken broth
1 pound raw shrimp (26-30 per pound), peeled and deveined, tails left on if desired

1/4 teaspoon freshly ground pepper
Pinch of salt
1 teaspoon oregano
1 teaspoon basil
2 tablespoons lemon juice
1/3 cup grated parmesan cheese
1/3 cup grated romano cheese
1/3 cup grated mozzarella cheese

Directions

> Pour 1 tablespoon oil and add gnocchi to skillet and heat the pan. Cook anywhere between 5 and 10 minutes. Make sure you stirring continuously. Then place in clean container.

> Pour the oil and add shallots to the same pan. Keep the heat on medium and cook for a few minutes, stirring occasionally. Add the asparagus and pour in broth and let cook covered for several more minutes. Add shrimp, spices, salt and pepper. Re-cover and bring to a simmer for another few minutes. Check that the shrimp is cooked!

> Pour in the lemon juice, and the gnocchi back to the skillet and pour. Cook and stir for just a couple of minutes then take away from heat and use all cheeses to smother the top. Cover and simmer until cheese has melted.
> Yummy for your tummy! ;)

Nutritional Facts:

Serving size 448 g, amount per serving, calories 400, calories from fat 120, total fat 13.4g, saturated fat 4.6g, trans fat 0.0g, cholesterol 254mg, sodium 642mg, potassium 1022mg, total carbohydrates 30.9g, dietary fiber 5.1g, sugars 3.3g, protein 40.1g

Low in sugar, high in phosphorus, high in vitamin b12, high in vitamin c

SEARED JALAPEÑO SALMON SNAP PEA SLAW

Say that five times fast! It's a mouthful, and so is this dish. The flavors are wonderful together: jalapeno, cilantro, ginger, lime, and rice vinegar. Salmon of course is one of the most savory fish to cook as well! This course takes little time to prepare which is good because your mouth will be watering until it is served.

Prep time: 10 minutes
Cook time: 5 minutes
Servings: 4

Ingredients

8 oz. Snap peas, trimmed and sliced
.5 oz. Jalapeño (about 1/2 - red and chopped)
3 tbsp. Fresh cilantro, chopped
1 tbsp. Fresh ginger, grated
1 tbsp. Fresh lemon juice

1 tbsp. Rice vinegar
1 tbsp. Olive oil
2 tsp. Soy sauce
Kosher salt
Freshly ground black pepper
4 salmon fillets.

Directions

> Add oil to a pan over medium high heat.
> Add the snap peas to the pan then mix in the red jalapeño, fresh cilantro, fresh ginger, and lastly pour in the fresh lemon juice, rice vinegar, canola oil, and soy sauce.
> While the slaw is cooking, sear the salmon.
> Use the salt and pepper to season the slaw.

Nutrition facts:

Serving size 254 g, amount per serving, calories 322, calories from fat 134, total fat 14.8g, saturated fat 2.2g, trans fat 0.0g, cholesterol 78mg, sodium 271mg, potassium 862mg, total carbohydrates 9.7g, dietary fiber 3.2g, sugars 3.5g. Protein 38.0gvery high in magnesium, very high in phosphorus, very high in selenium, high in vitamin c

TANTALIZING TILAPIA IN GARLIC AND FRESH TOMATOES

One of the most basic and adaptable fish, tilapia can be easily acquired and cooked into a savory meal. With this particular entrée the fish is soaked and seared in tomato, wine, olive, and garlic. Many of the ingredients are common and can be found in most kitchens, but make sure to buy enough wine for the fish and you to share! Quick and easy!

Prep time: 10 minutes
Cook time: 10 minutes
Servings: 4

Ingredients

1 1/4 pounds tilapia
1/4 teaspoon salt
1/4 teaspoon freshly ground pepper
3 tablespoons cilantro
2.5 oz. Lime (fresh zest and juice.)

2 tablespoons extra-virgin olive oil, divided
1 pint grape or cherry tomatoes, halved if large
1/4 cup dry white wine
3 cloves garlic, finely chopped

Directions

> Season the fish with salt, pepper, cilantro, and zest of lime.
> Add 1 tablespoon oil in a skillet over medium-high heat. Cook the fish half way the turn on other side, about 5 minutes or so, then transfer the tilapia to a clean plate and place under foil. You can add a pinch or salt and pepper just for hint of flavor.
> Add the rest of the ingredients after turning off the heat to the pan. Cover on medium heat; cook the mixture for no more than 5 minutes, stirring occasionally. Pour the sauce over the fish. Add parsley garnish if desired.

Nutritional Facts:

Serving size 231 g, amount per serving, calories 229, calories from fat 76, total fat 8.5g, saturated fat 1.6g, trans fat 0.0g, cholesterol 69mg, sodium 200mg, potassium 135mg, total carbohydrates 11.0g, dietary fiber 1.0g, sugars 7.9g, protein 27.0g

PAN-FRIED GARLIC PARMESEAN TUNA CAKES

That's right, not crab cakes, but tuna cakes! Though the maryland delicacy is a great entrée, there can be variations within the seafood family. These tuna patties are perfect for dinner and also for lunch, and are easy enough to make at any time for you or a group. Dip in some hot sauce for extra spicy flavor!

Prep time: 15 minutes
Cook time: 10 minutes
Servings: 8

Ingredients

2 eggs
2 teaspoons lemon juice
¾ cup bread crumbs (italian seasoned)
3 (6 oz) cans tuna, drained
¼ cup diced onion

2 cloves of garlic, minced
1 teaspoon oregano
1 teaspoon basil
1 pinch ground black pepper
3 tablespoons olive oil

Directions

> To make the paste, whisk the eggs in a small container along with the lemon juice together before stirring in the bread crumbs and parmesan cheese. Add onions and garlic, stir, and then fold in tuna until mixed is combined. Season the fish with black pepper, oregano, and basil, and then separate into about 8 full sized patties.

> Add oil to skillet and fry each patty...each side will be about 4-5 minutes; you will know when they are done when you see them turn a light crisp brown in color.

Nutritional Facts:

Serving size 96 g, amount per serving, calories 223, calories from fat 109, total fat 12.1g, saturated fat 2.3g, cholesterol 61mg, sodium 122mg, potassium 260mg, total carbohydrates 8.1g, dietary fiber 0.7g, sugars 0.9g, protein 19.8g

Low in sugar, high in niacin, very high in selenium, high in vitamin b12

RED HOT GARLIC PARMESAN SHRIMP SKILLET PASTA

There are not too many ways to go wrong with shrimp and this recipe isn't one of them. Pairing spinach, basil, sweet peas and pesto make a great and easy italian dish

Prep time: 5 minutes
Cook time: 35 minutes
Servings: 8

Ingredients

12oz rotini pasta (can substitute with penne pasta)
1oz parmesan cheese (grated)
¼ cup pine nuts
1 chopped clove garlic
1 tsp. Sea salt

1 tsp. Freshly ground black pepper
1 lb. Shrimp (peeled and deveined medium)
1 cup peas
Pinch of crushed red pepper
1 tsp. Chili flakes for garnish

Directions

> Prepare pesto in a food blender for an easy mix: add spinach, basil, parmesan cheese, pine nuts, garlic crushed red pepper, salt and pepper.
> Add shrimp to a non-stick skillet and cook for 4 minutes or till you see the shrimp is cooked.
> Add cooked pasta, peas and pesto. Combine ¼ cup water to skillet stirring occasionally until the sauce richens up.
> Garnish with cheese, chili flakes and serve.

Nutritional Facts:

Serving size 126 g, amount per serving, calories 246, calories from fat 51, total fat 5.7g, saturated fat 1.2g, trans fat 0.0g, cholesterol 153mg, sodium 418mg, potassium 248mg, total carbohydrates 27.8g, dietary fiber 1.2g, sugars 1.2g, protein 20.5g

Low in sugar, high in phosphorus

ITALIAN BASIL FRIED FISH

Ever fried fish in a skillet without oil or butter? With the non-stick pan you don't need butter or oil. This is an easy way to re-create a dish with delicious taste

Prep time: 5 minutes
Cook time: 25 minutes
Servings: 4

Ingredients

1 tbsp. Traditional basil pesto sauce
1 chopped yellow pepper
1 chopped zucchini

1 cup grape tomatoes
3 tbsp. Diced fresh basil

Directions

> Dress the fish with dressing.
> Add fish to a non-stick skillet and cook for 3 minutes on each side. (you will see the fish start to flake when done)
> Move to plate and make sure to keep the fish warm.
> Add pesto, vegetables and the rest of the dressing, to the skillet. Keep stirring and cook for about five minutes.
> Garnish with basil and serve over cooked pasta.

Nutritional Facts:

Serving size 146 g, amount per serving, calories 46, calories from fat 17, total fat 1.9g, trans fat 0.0g, cholesterol 1mg, sodium 32mg, potassium 339mg, total carbohydrates 6.6g, dietary fiber 1.6g, sugars 2.3g, protein 1.9g

Very low in cholesterol, high in dietary fiber, high in manganese, high in magnesium, very high in potassium, very high in vitamin a, very high in vitamin b6, very high in vitamin c

KICKIN ARTIC CHAR

Char is a great substitute for salmon or trout, especially for those who want to protect the environment. For those who like mild types of fish, this is the recipe for you, and you can finish it off with a kick.

Prep time: 5 minutes
Cook time: 30 minutes
Servings: 4

Ingredients

1/4 cup shallots (large diced)
1 cup chicken broth
1/4 cup water
1 lb. Chopped kale
1 lb. Arctic char (skinned & cut into 4 portions)

1/4 tsp. Salt
1/4 tsp. Freshly ground pepper
1/4 cup reduced-fat sour cream
2 tsp. Prepared horseradish
1 tbsp. Chopped fresh dill
4 lemon wedges for garnish

Directions

> Create sauce: combine dill, horseradish and sour cream in a mixing bowl.
> Add shallots to a non-stick pan and cook for 2 minutes.
> Next, add the broth, water and half the kale and cook for 10 minutes.
> Season the fish with salt and pepper and add to the skillet. Cook for 7 minutes.
> Serve the fish over cooked pasta, with the sauce and garnish with lemon wedges.

Nutritional Facts:

Serving size 330 g, amount per serving, calories 283, calories from fat 79, total fat 8.8g, saturated fat 3.3g, trans fat 0.0g, cholesterol 101mg, sodium 494mg, potassium 697mg, total carbohydrates 15.2g, dietary fiber 1.9g, protein 8.2g

Very low in sugar, high in manganese, very high in vitamin a, very high in vitamin c

SANTA CRUZ STYLE CLAMBAKE

This is a perfect recipe for those who are craving a beachside classic. The clambake is not reserved to when you go to the seashore, but can be made right here, "right now" in your very own kitchen anytime.

Prep time: 20 minutes
Cook time: 20 minutes
Servings: 4

Ingredients

3 cups water
1 tablespoon seafood seasoning
1 dozen red potatoes (12 potatos)
3 ears fresh corn

1 tsp. Salt
2 dozen cleaned littleneck clams (2 lbs.)
1/4 cup melted butter
Parsley for garnish

Directions

> In a non-stick skillet add water, seasoning, potatoes, corn and salt and cook for 20 min.
> Add clams, cover and cook for 5 minutes. (when clams are ready they will open!)
> Warning: throw away any clams that do not open.
> Garnish with parsley and serve with melted butter.

Nutritional Facts:

serving size 1116 g, amount per serving, calories 706, calories from fat 119, total fat 13.3g, saturated fat 7.6g, cholesterol 31mg, sodium 1529mg, potassium 3263mg, total carbohydrates 138.1g, dietary fiber 13.5g, sugars 15.6g, protein 15.2g

Low in cholesterol, high in potassium, very high in vitamin b6, high in vitamin c

HERB CRUSTED COD WITH VEGETABLES

This is a fast and easy dinner that you can make on a regular basis. The kids will love the flavor and you will enjoy the small clean-up. It's a win-win for everyone.

Prep time: 15 minutes
Cook time: 15 minutes
Servings: 4

Ingredients

1/4 cup water
2 tsps. Dry white wine
1/2 teaspoon thyme
Ground black pepper
1 large diced carrot

2 stalks diced celery
1 diced small onion
1 can condensed cream of mushroom soup
4 firm cod fillets

Directions

> In a non-stick pan bring the water and wine to a boil.
> Then add thyme, black pepper, carrot, celery and onion
> Cover and simmer for 5 minutes.
> Add the soup, and the fish to the skillet. Put the lid on the skillet and cook for 5 more minutes.
> Garnish and serve.

There is no nutritional facts for this recipe

SPICED HALIBUT WITH CORN SUCCOTASH

Halibut with corn succotash is a refreshing summer dish to cook on a hot day when you want to mix what it is in season. This dish will not disappoint. Light...healthy and delicious!

Prep time: 15 minutes
Cook time: 15 minutes
Servings: 4

Ingredients

12 oz can whole kernel corn,
2 peppers (red and green - mix with corn)
2 tsps. Sliced green onions (2 medium)
2 tsps. Chopped fresh cilantro
½ tsp. Ground cumin
1 tsp. Lime juice

1 tsp. Honey
¼ tsp. Ground cumin
1/8 tsp. Pepper
1/8 tsp. Sea salt
4 halibut fillet

Directions

> Prepare succotash: pour all succotash ingredients into a mixing bowl.
> Cover the fish in cumin adding salt and pepper on both sides.
> In a non-stick skillet cook the fish for 4 minutes on each side till it starts browning and flakes easily.
> Garnish and serve with succotash mixture...yummy!

Nutritional Facts:

Serving size 157 g, amount per serving, calories 406, calories from fat 67, total fat 7.4g, saturated fat 1.0g, cholesterol 93mg, sodium 218mg, potassium 1623mg, total carbohydrates 21.1g, dietary fiber 3.1g, sugars 5.6g, protein 63.3g

Low in saturated fat, low in sodium, very high in iron, high in magnesium, very high in niacin, high in phosphorus, high in potassium, very high in selenium, very high in vitamin b6, very high in vitamin b12, very high in vitamin c

MEDITERRANEAN GARLIC JALAPENO WHITEFISH

This mediterranean garlic jalapeno whitefish is a nice-n-light, cool and refreshing dish. One that you can complete in no time.

Prep time: 30 minutes
Cook time: 30 minutes
Servings: 2

Ingredients

1 large diced tomato
1 diced small green pepper
1 diced jalapeno pepper
3 tsp. Chopped fresh basil
3 tsp. White wine or chicken broth

1 diced shallot
1 diced garlic clove
1 tbsp. Chili powder
2 whitefish fillets

Directions

> Prepare tomato mixture: combine tomatoes, peppers, basil, wine, shallot, garlic and chili powder in s mixing container.
> Season the fish with chili powder.
> In a non-stick skillet cook the fish (until brown and flakey) for 4 minutes on each side.
> Add the tomato mixture at the last 2 minutes of cooking.
> Garnish and serve.
>

Nutritional Facts:

Serving size 302 g, amount per serving, calories 257, calories from fat 76, total fat 8.4g, saturated fat 1.5g, cholesterol 31mg, sodium 507mg, potassium 1394mg, total, carbohydrates 36.2g, dietary fiber 18.5g, sugars 9.2g
Protein 20.4g

Very high in dietary fiber, high in iron, high in manganese, high in magnesium, high in niacin, high in phosphorus, high in potassium, high in selenium, very high in vitamin a, very high in vitamin b6, very high in vitamin c

PORK:

Pork...the other white meat! You know, a lot of people shy away from this delicious flavorful meat, but the reality is...this category of meat is probably the most flavorful of all! Whether cooking a entrée or just adding a little to a meal to give the most perfect flavor, or adding a savory twits to a dish...you will adore the recipes we have custom created for you and yours!

BAKED HOT ITALIAN SAUSAGE, FOUR CHEESY ROTONI

You're in the mood for some of grandma's home cooking, but you don't want to slave in the kitchen all day long. Then this dish is perfect for you and your family. It's taking a memory from your childhood and putting your own spin on it, without compromising on the taste. That's the most important part after all.

Prep time: 10 minutes
Cook time: 10 minutes
Servings: 8

Ingredients

1-pound rotini (penne pasta if desired)
3/4 pound hot italian sausage
2 sweet red peppers
1 onion (see note)
26 ounces marinara sauce (1 jar)

2 cups shredded italian four-cheese blend
Tablespoon of basil
Pinch of crushed red peppers (to add a little kick!)

Directions -

> Cook pasta.
> Slice the sausage, peppers and onions and add to a non-stick skillet.
> Cook for 10 minutes adding the pinch of crushed red peppers.
> Add sauce and basil to the dish and simmer.
> Next, add in the drained pasta and the cheese.
> Bake in the oven at 425 degrees for 7 minutes.
> Cool and serve.

Nutritional Facts:

Serving size 263 g, amount per serving, calories 553, calories from fat 222, total fat 24.7g, saturated fat 10.6g, trans fat 0.1g, cholesterol 67mg, sodium 873mg, potassium 528mg, total carbohydrates 58.2g, dietary fiber 5.3g, sugars 11.5g, protein 24.7g

High in vitamin c

SPICY SKILLET PORK & BACON FRIED RICE

In the mood for asian tonight, but don't want to order take out. Here is a way for you to learn how to make one of your favorite dishes, so that you can continue to make it over and over again.

Prep time: 15 minutes
Cook time: 15 minutes
Servings: 4

Ingredients

3/4 lb. Boneless pork loin
6oz bacon (6 slices)
1 onion diced or cut into strips
1 cup diced mushrooms
2 eggs

3 cups cold cooked rice
2 tablespoons soy sauce
3 tablespoons chicken broth
1 tablespoon of crushed red peppers

Directions

> In a non-stick skillet cook the pork and stir-fry until brown. Remove the pork.
> Cook onions and mushrooms for 5 minutes.
> Add beaten eggs to the skillet and cook until they start setting.
> Lastly, add the cooked pork, cooked bacon, rice, soy sauce, and broth to skillet and cook for 6 minutes or until you see the eggs start to texture.
> Garnish and add fresh ground pepper for added flavor...serve.

Nutritional Facts:

Serving size 354 g, amount per serving, calories 915, calories from fat 218, total fat 24.2g, saturated fat 7.8g, trans fat 0.0g, cholesterol 191mg, sodium 1558mg, potassium 937mg, total carbohydrates 116.3g, dietary fiber 3.0g, sugars 2.1g, protein 52.4g

Very low in sugar, high in selenium, high in thiamin, high in vitamin b6

SWEET AND SAVORY GARLIC PORK

This is a perfect meal to make your kids fall in love with their vegetables. The mouthwatering pork, paired with soy sauce will give that salted pork taste that everyone loves.

Prep time: 20 minutes
Cook time: 20 minutes
Servings: 4

Ingredients

1 lb. Pork tenderloin, cut into strips
16 oz. Stir fry vegetables (yellow, red and green peppers, onions)
1/4 cup sesame oil (asian toasted dressing)

2 tbsp. Soy sauce
1/2 tsp. Garlic powder
2 cups broccoli slaw

Directions

> In a non-stick skillet add the stripped pork tenderloin and cook for 5 minutes till it is cooked through.
> Add stir-fry and cook for 5 more minutes.
> Pour in soy sauce, dressing, garlic powder and cook for 2 minutes.
> Turn off heat and pour in broccoli and serve.

Nutritional Facts:

Serving size 294 g, amount per serving, calories 342, calories from fat 160, total fat 17.8g, saturated fat 3.3g, trans fat 0.0g, cholesterol 83mg, sodium 546mg, potassium 872mg, total carbohydrates 11.5g, dietary fiber 4.3g, sugars 4.1g, protein 33.0g

High in niacin, very high in selenium, very high in thiamin, very high in vitamin a, high in vitamin b6, very high in vitamin c

HAWAIIN PINAPPLE SAUTEED PORK

Experience the taste of the islands from your very own kitchen. Teaming pineapples, and thyme together will make you feel like you are strolling on the beach and have your taste-buds screaming for more.

Prep time: 30 minutes
Cook time: 30 minutes
Servings: 4

Ingredients

1oz pineapple jam (3 tablespoons preserves)

3 tablespoons orange juice

2 teaspoons dijon mustard

1/2 teaspoon minced fresh ginger

1/2 teaspoon curry powder

8 oz pineapples (4 fresh or canned pineapple rings - 1/2 inch-thick and cut in half, save any remaining juice)

4 5 ounce boneless pork loin chops (1/2 inch thick), trimmed

2 tablespoons chopped fresh thyme (see tip), divided

1/2 teaspoon salt, divided

1/4 teaspoon freshly ground pepper, divided

Directions

> Create sauce: preserves, orange juice, mustard, ginger and curry powder in a mixing bowl. Set aside.
> Add the pork chops into non-stick skillet and cover with thyme, salt and pepper.
> Cook for 3 minutes on each side.
> Pour the preserve juice and cook for 3 minutes longer.
> Transfer to a plate.
> Add the pineapple and the sauce to the pan. Cook for 2 minutes.
> Serve on top of the pork.

Nutritional Facts:

Serving size 222 g, amount per serving, calories 263, calories from fat 48, total fat 5.3g, saturated fat 1.8g, trans fat 0.1g, cholesterol 103mg, sodium 404mg, potassium 710mg, total carbohydrates 14.9g, dietary fiber 1.6g, sugars 10.1g, protein 37.8g

High in manganese, very high in niacin, high in phosphorus, high in riboflavin, very high in selenium, very high in thiamin, very high in vitamin b6, very high in vitamin c

HONEY CRUNCH PECAN PORK

It's one of those school nights and you have to whip up something fast and delicious that the whole family will love? Well, then this is the recipe for you. This skillet fried pork cutlets are super-fast to make and will leave you licking your plate and asking for more.

Prep time: 15 minutes
Cook time: 15 minutes
Servings: 4

Ingredients

1/3 cup all-purpose flour
1 teaspoon salt
1/2 teaspoon black pepper
20oz boneless pork loin chops (4 average pork chops)
4 tablespoons butter, divided

1/4 cup finely chopped onion
1oz pecans (chopped)
1/4 cup honey
1/4 cup chicken broth
1 teaspoon lemon juice

Directions

> Cover the pork in the flour, salt and pepper. (meat prep)
> Add the pork to a non-stick skillet and cook for 4-5 minutes on each side until it starts to get a little crispy.
> Transfer to a plate and keep warm.
> Add the butter, onions, and pecans for 6 minutes.
> Add the rest of the ingredients and cook for several minutes more simmering.
> Serve with sauce over the top of the pork chops.

Excellent dish to dip sourdough bread with!

Nutritional Facts:

Serving size 220 g, amount per serving, calories 462, calories from fat 196, total fat 21.8g, saturated fat 9.5g, trans fat 0.1g, cholesterol 134mg, sodium 793mg, potassium 680mg, total carbohydrates 27.4g, dietary fiber 1.3g, sugars 18.1g, protein 39.5g
High in niacin, very high in selenium, very high in thiamin, high in vitamin b6

THE AMAZING TABASCO PORK AND BEANS SKILLET

The amazing tabasco pork and beans skillet is a one skillet meal. This is a dish where you can add all of your ingredients to one skillet and it not only builds flavor, but it makes for an easy clean up!

Prep time: 10 minutes
Cook time: 10 minutes
Servings: 2

Ingredients

1/2-pound boneless pork chops, 3/4-inch-thick (about 2 chops)
1/3 cup chopped onion
1/3 cup chopped celery

16 oz) of pork and beans (1 can)
2 teaspoons packed brown sugar
1 tablespoon tabasco sauce
Parsley for garnish

Directions

> In a non-stick skillet cook the pork chops for 10 minutes or till they start to crisp.
> Transfer pork chops to a plate then and cook the celery and onion for 2 minutes.
> Stir in the pork and beans, and brown sugar and tabasco sauce. Bring to a boil.
> Return the pork chops, cover and simmer for 5 minutes.
> Garnish with parsley and serve.

Nutritional Facts:

Serving size 386 g, amount per serving, calories 255calories from fat 39, total fat 4.4g, saturated fat 1.4g, trans fat 0.0g, cholesterol 83mg, sodium 139mg, potassium 1037mg, total carbohydrates 21.5g, dietary fiber 8.4g, sugars 7.1g, protein 34.2g

High in dietary fiber, high in niacin, high in phosphorus, high in potassium, high in riboflavin, very high in selenium, very high in thiamin, high in vitamin a, very high in vitamin b6, very high in vitamin c

PO' BOY PORK RAMON SKILLET

Don't know what to do with all those ramen noodles in your dorm room. This recipe pairs ramen noodles, with the flavors of pork and fresh stir-fried veggies, so well that you won't realize that you are still living on a budget.

Prep time: 10 minutes
Cook time: 10 minutes
Servings: 4

Ingredients

¾ pound pork tenderloin, cut into 1/8-inch strips
6 ounces egg noodles
1 ½ cups water
1 medium red bell pepper, cut into 3/4 inch pieces (1 cup)

1 cup broccoli (flowerets)
4 medium green onions, cut into 1-inch pieces (1/2 cup)
1 tbsp. Parsley (chopped fresh or 2 teaspoons parsley flakes, if desired)
1 tablespoon soy sauce

Directions

> Add pork to a non-stick skillet and cook for 6 minutes or till cooked stirring occasionally.
> Add broken noodles, and rest of ingredients into the skillet.
> Bring to a boil and add only 1 packet of the roman seasoning to the pan and cook for 5 minutes.
> Garnish and serve.

Nutritional Facts:

Serving size 289 g, amount per serving, calories 205calories from fat 37, total fat 4.1g, saturated fat 1.2g, trans fat 0.0g, cholesterol 74mg, sodium 290mg, potassium 565mg, total carbohydrates 15.5g, dietary fiber 2.2g, sugars 2.2g, protein 25.7g

High in niacin, high in phosphorus, high in riboflavin, very high in selenium, very high in thiamin, high in vitamin a, high in vitamin b6, very high in vitamin c

HEARTY ONE-POT SAUSAGE & BROCCOLI SCALLOPED POTATOES

Only one piece of kitchenware is needed for this delicious dish. Your parents always told you to eat your broccoli, and you are, but there are pleasing additions like potatoes, salsa, and sausage to go along with the famed vegetable. This entrée is very easy to prepare and in the end you have a complete meal to share with the family or friends!

Prep time: 10 minutes
Cook time: 30 minutes
Servings: 6

Ingredients

5 oz scalloped potatoes (1 box)
2 cups hot water
2/3 cup milk
2 tablespoons margarine or butter
1lb kielbasa sausage (sliced fully cooked from 1-lb ring)

½ cup salsa (any variety)
2 cups broccoli (frozen florets)
4 cloves garlic, minced
1 tablespoon chives
1/3 cup grated cheddar cheese

Directions

> In a skillet or pan, bring to a boil the potatoes, sauce mix, hot water, milk, margarine, garlic, and chives, stirring occasionally the mixture.
> Mix in the sausage and salsa then lower the heat. Simmer for 15-20 minutes with the pan covered, stirring every so often. You should see the sauce thicken a little more as it's cooking.
> Add the cheese and broccoli and stir. Re-cover and cook for 6-8 minutes. The sauce should richen up even more upon cooking and the vegetables cook to their right texture.

Nutritional Facts:

Serving size 336 g, amount per serving, calories 407, calories from fat 255, total fat 28.4g, saturated fat 9.4g, trans fat 0.2g, cholesterol 73mg, sodium 816mg34%, potassium 732mg21%, total carbohydrates 18.0g, dietary fiber 3.0g, sugars 3.9g, protein 20.2g

High in vitamin b6, high in vitamin c

FRESH AND TENDER "ISLAND THYME" PORK

Though most fantasize about spending time on the beach, drinking fruity cocktails, and eating juicy and fresh cuisine, it is possible to have an island meal at home. The pineapple, apricot, and orange seep into the meat, and the curry cures your island fever. This course has all the right spices, especially the sprinkle of thyme that brings the whole meal together in the end!

Prep time: 30 minutes
Cook time: 15 minutes
Servings: 4

Ingredients

2 tablespoons pineapple jam (preserves)
1 tablespoon orange marmalade
3 tablespoons orange juice, plus more if needed
1/2 teaspoon minced fresh ginger
1/2 teaspoon curry powder
3.5 oz pineapple rings (4 fresh rings or canned 1/2 inch thick, cut in half, any juice reserved)

2 teaspoons butter
4 5 ounce pork loin chops (boneless 1/2 inch thick), trimmed
2 tablespoons chopped fresh thyme, divided
1/2 teaspoon salt, divided
1/4 teaspoon freshly ground pepper, divided
1 oz cilantro

Directions

> Mix the pineapple reserves, orange marmalade, 3 tablespoons ginger, orange juice, and curry powder and set aside until needed. Also...set aside enough orange juice to the pineapple juice...orange juice should be about 1/3 cup total..
> Melt butter in a large nonstick skillet over medium-high heat. Season the pork chops with 1/4 teaspoon salt, 1/8 teaspoon pepper and about 1/2 tablespoon thyme, on each side then add to skillet. Cook on one side for a few minutes then turn on other side after you see them brown.

> Lower the heat on the stove (around medium) and add the rest of the juice you put to the side. Cook the chops for a few minutes before move over to a clean plate; cover with foil.
> Using the same pan, cook pineapple, reserved sauce and the rest of the thyme for only a minute or two.
> Cover the pork and pineapple with however much sauce you desire; garnish with cilantro. (can also garnish with parsley for cilantro substitute, if desired)

Nutritional Facts:
Serving size 205 g, amount per serving, calories 535, calories from fat 336, total fat 37.4g, saturated fat 14.5g, trans fat 0.0g, cholesterol 127mg, sodium 414mg, potassium 605mg, total carbohydrates 16.2g, dietary fiber 1.4g, sugars 11.4g, protein 32.5g

High in selenium, high in thiamin

BROILED AND BRAISED TENDERLOIN
WITH FRESH MANGO SALSA

There's just something about pork and fruit that goes well together. The juices of both complement each other, and it's very apparent in this caribbean-influenced entrée. Mango and lime add citrus to the spices and the tenderloin is cooked to be just as juicy as its marinade. A light and quick dinner for a breezy summer evening!

Prep time: 10 minutes
Cook time: 25 minutes
Servings: 4

Ingredients
1 mango, chopped
2 scallions, chopped
1 tablespoon plus 1 teaspoon oil
1lime, zest and juice
1/2 lemon, zest and juice

1/4teaspoon crushed red pepper
Kosher salt
1 1/4 pounds pork tenderloin 1 tenderloin)
1teaspoon ground coriander

Directions
> Heat broiler.
> Mix together 1 tablespoon of the oil, mango, scallions, lime zest and juice, lemon zest and juice, crushed red pepper, and a pinch of salt then put this mixture to the side and save for later.
> Over the meat pour a teaspoon of oil and spread around the meat. After that you will season with coriander and a couple pinches of teaspoon of salt.
> Place the pork in the broiler for 6-7 minutes on each side. Make sure you check the meat to see if it is browning before you turn it over to its other. Repeat the process.
> Give the meat about 5 minutes to cool before slicing, and serve with the salsa mixture.
> Delicious recipe that is simple and a ton of flavor.

Nutritional Facts:

Serving size 77 g, amount per serving, calories 82, calories from fat 43, total fat 4.7g, saturated fat 0.6, trans fat 0.0g, cholesterol 0mg, sodium 41mg, potassium 121mg, total carbohydrates 10.4g, dietary fiber 1.5g. Sugars 8.0g, protein 0.6g

No cholesterol, low in sodium, high in vitamin a, very high in vitamin c

SIZZLING & SPICY HONEY JALAPENO SPINACH PORK

These pork wraps are a multipurpose dish; they can either be served as an appetizer or a main course, depending on how hungry you are! The chili paste and jalapeno add plenty of spice, and with the addition of spinach, the dish becomes healthier without losing any of the great flavors within the stir-fry. A win-win!

Prep time: 30 minutes
Cook time: 15 minutes
Servings: 4

Ingredients

3/4 lb. Boneless pork loin, cut into 1/4" by 2" strips
1/2 large red pepper, cut into strips
1/2 cup fresh bean spouts
1/3 cup fresh leek strips
1 large jalapeño pepper, trimmed, seeded and diced

1 tbsp. Hot chili paste with garlic
1 teaspoon cayenne pepper
1 tbsp. Rice wine vinegar
4 tbsp. Soy sauce
1 tbsp. Honey
1 cup baby spinach
1/3 cup peanuts, chopped (optional)

Directions

> Set washed spinach on a serving plate either as a bed or around the side.
> Except for the spinach and peanuts, combine all the ingredients in a bowl, or mixing container. Refrigerate so the meat can marinate for about an hour. (you can marinade longer to have the juices set in the meat even deeper)
> When you're ready to start cooking, remove the bowl and sit it out for approximately 15 minutes or till the meat is at room temperature.
> Add ingredients to a preheated pan on medium-high heat preferably. The meat is done when it has started to brown, but cook to desired doneness. (the longer you cook the more brown it will become) then add the meat on the of spinach. If you wish you can sprinkle and garnish the dish with chopped nuts. (add a parsley garnish if desired as well for an extra color to the dish.)

Nutrition facts:

Serving size 165 g, amount per serving, calories 245, calories from fat 88, total fat 9.8g, saturated fat 1.9g, trans fat 0.0g, cholesterol 63mg, sodium 1006mg. Potassium 596mg, total carbohydrates 12.0g, dietary fiber 2.1g, sugars 7.4g, protein 27.3g

High in niacin, high in phosphorus, very high in selenium, very high in thiamin, high in vitamin a, high in vitamin b6, very high in vitamin c

SOUPS

Oh yeah...we've got soups! 'this section of deliciousness will take you back to the days that mom used to "work it" in the kitchen! These succulent soups will have you on the next level of cravings! The great thing about soup is that you can add a little bit more of that seasoning that is your go to in the kitchen. See how you can mix it up and "get jiggy wit it" with these mouth-watering soups that will have your friends & family clapping for joy!

GOOEY GRILLED CHEESE MINIS IN CREAMY TOMATO SOUP

What is the go-to meal when you can't think of anything and are short on food? Grilled cheese, of course. Imagine actually preparing for the delicious backup plan now. A simple dish can be altered to something amazing with a little patience and preparation. Plus, when will there be a better time to make small grilled cheese sandwiches floating atop tomato soup? Actually, probably all of the time.

Prep time: 10 minutes
Cook time: 40 minutes
Servings: 6

Ingredients

3 tablespoons olive oil
2 yellow onions, chopped
3 cloves garlic (minced)
4 cups chicken stock
1 (28-ounce) can crushed tomatoes
1 tablespoon oregano
1 tablespoon basil
2 tablespoon sea salt

1 teaspoon freshly ground black pepper
1/2 cup orzo
1/2 cup heavy cream

Grilled cheese croutons:
5 oz wheat bread (4 slices country wheat)
2 tablespoons unsalted butter, melted
4 ounces cheddar cheese, grated

Directions

> Add olive oil to a large pan and heat on about medium for a couple of minutes. Lower the heat just a tad and cook the onions for 12-14 and keep stirring till it starts to brown in the pan, then mix in the garlic

> Cook this for an additional minute. After the garlic and onion have cooked, add the chicken stock, tomatoes, oregano, basil, 1 tablespoon salt and 1 teaspoon pepper and stir till the soup starts to boil. Cook on low for about 12-14 min. After lowering the heat.

> While this is taking place, boil water and a few pinches of salt in another pan. Cook the orzo for 5-6 minutes, drain, and add to the soup (don't worry about the orzo being done

when you drain it...while it is cooking in the soup it will finish cooking). Add cream stirring occasionally and cook the soup for about 7-9 minutes. (make sure you keep stirring the soup while it is cooking)

Grilled cheese croutons
> Place the four slices of buttered bread in a skillet, buttered side down. Pile cheddar on two of the slices and the place the others on top of the cheese, buttered side up. Grill for just a couple of minutes each side, flipping the sandwiches halfway. (make sure not to burn the bread)
> After letting sit for 1 minutes, cut the grilled cheese up into little squares and let the squares float on top of the soup.

Nutritional Facts:
Serving size 419 g, amount per serving, calories 396, calories from fat 201, total fat 22.4g, saturated fat 10.0g, trans fat 0.2g, cholesterol 44mg, sodium 2897mg121%, potassium 173mg, total carbohydrates 36.6g, dietary fiber 7.6g, sugars 11.7g, protein 14.1g

Vitamin a 37%, vitamin c 22%, calcium 27%, iron 20%, nutrition grade c+, based on a 2000 calorie diet

JAMBALAYA FOR JOY

We look towards the bayou for this classic creole dish. The wonderful thing about jambalaya is that there are thousands of variations and depending on the person, each and every one of them is enjoyable! It is a one-pot mixture of essentials: meat, vegetables, and grains. This dish is a meal in its own that everyone can be satisfied with.

Prep time: 20 minutes
Cook time: 1 hour
Servings: 6

Ingredients

1 lb. Chicken breasts, cut into bite-size pieces
1 lb. Sausage, cut into ¼-inch thick slices
1/4 tbsp. Olive oil
1/2 c. Onion, chopped
1/2 c shallots
1 large bell pepper, chopped
2 cloves of garlic, minced

1 - 14.5 oz can diced tomatoes (do not drain)
1 1/2 c. Chicken stock
1 c rice
1/2 tsp. Dried thyme
1 tbsp. Parsley
1 tsp. Paprika
1 tsp. Chili powder

Directions

> Add olive oil to a sauté pan over medium heat and then place the sausage and chicken until the chicken is done.
> Remove the meat from the pan, and then add the onion, shallot, bell pepper and garlic; cook this sizzling mixture until onion is tender, adding the chicken broth, diced tomatoes, thyme, paprika, chili powder, parsley, and bay leaves. (you can add a teaspoon of crushed red peppers to heat things up just a bit)
> Lower the heat and cover cooking for approximately 18-20 minutes.
> Mix in rice and the meat that had been set aside. Make heat into a slow boil and cover for another 18-20 minutes.
> Season to taste with a little salt and pepper. (you can keep the bay leaf in to keep the flavor going)

Nutritional Facts:

Serving size 301 g, amount per serving, calories 547, calories from fat 254, total fat 28.2g, saturated fat 8.6g, trans fat 0.2g, cholesterol 131mg, sodium 842mg, potassium 586mg, total carbohydrates 30.7g, dietary fiber 1.6g, sugars 2.0g, protein 39.9g

Low in sugar, high in niacin, high in vitamin c

GARLIC & WATER CHESTNUT CHICKEN NOODLE SOUP

Just like grandma used to make! This one is the "throwback" of the recipes in this book. Who doesn't love the savory flavor of some good chicken noodle soup. Remember, you can add crackers to this amazing dish., or just dip in some grilled cheese, get the picture?

Prep time: 20 minutes
Cook time: 20 minutes
Servings: 4-6

Ingredients

1 tablespoon butter
1/2 cup diced carrot
1/2 cup diced onion
1/2 cup diced celery
1 tablespoon garlic powder
1 tablespoon parsley
1/8 cup diced water chestnuts

1 pinch salt
1/4 teaspoon fresh thyme leaves
2 quarts roasted chicken broth
4 ounces uncooked wide egg noodles
2 cooked boneless chicken breast halves
Cubed 1 pinch cayenne pepper (optional)
1 pinch salt & ground black pepper to taste

Directions

> Stir in the butter, carrot, onion, garlic powder, celery, parsley, water chestnuts, salt, and fresh thyme in a large pot over medium heat. Keep stirring everything until the onions start to turn wilted and a little see through. At least 5 minutes.
> Bring chicken broth to bring to a boil while stirring.
> Cook the egg noodles until tender, approximately 5 minutes, stirring occasionally.
> Last, stir in cooked chicken breast. Turn heat down to a simmer. 5-6 minutes.
> To add a little heat, add cayenne pepper, salt and black pepper for flavor.

Nutritional Facts:

Serving size 5 (500g), calories 297, total fat 7.7g, saturated fat 3g, trans fat 0g, cholesterol 84mg, sodium 1271mg, potassium 613mg, total carb 21.3g, dietary fiber 1.7g, sugars 3.1g , protein 33.2g

THICK-N-HEARTY GARLIC LINTEL SOUP

With a bowl of this soup, it's like a meal of its own! You will indulge yourself with this hearty meal that will feed an army! These combination of flavors will make your mouth water just when reading the directions. This one is one of our favorites and i'm sure it will soon be yours! Dig in! ;)

Prep time: 12 minutes
Cook time: 1 hour
Servings: 6-8

Ingredients

2 carrots, diced
2 stalks celery, chopped
2 cloves garlic, minced
1 onion, chopped
1/4 cup olive oil
1 teaspoon dried oregano
1 bay leaf

1 teaspoon dried basil
1 (14.5 ounce) can crushed tomatoes
2 cups dry lentils
8 cups water
1/2 cup spinach, rinsed and thinly sliced
2 tablespoons vinegar salt to taste ground
black pepper to taste

Directions

> Heat oil over medium heat in a large pan. Add celery, onions, carrots and garlic. Keep cook for about 2-3 minutes.
> Stir in onion and cook till soft.
> Stir in garlic, bay leaf, oregano, and basil and cayenne pepper and cook for 3-4 minutes.
> Add water and tomatoes, then stir in lentils. Reduce heat after it starts to boil
> Simmer for at approximately 1 hour. Before it's served stir in spinach but make sure to cook into soup until it starts to break down. Add vinegar, and flavor to to your liking..

Nutritional Facts:

Serving size 8 (383g), calories 248, total fat 7g, saturated fat 1g, trans fat 0g, cholesterol 0mg, sodium 29mg   , potassium 682mg, total carb 34.2g, dietary fiber 16.1g, sugars 3.8g, protein 13.3g

APPETIZERS:

Well now...the beauty about this section is that it's all about the munchies! Appetizers are a great way to start up the party and get things going with the family, friends and company! We have a lot in store for you in this next section for you to ponder and munch on. Feel free to add a little more garlic and some of your own flavorful delights as you make some of these favorites your own! See what you can create and how you will start to dazzle the taste buds of your family, company and friends! Now it's time to "throw down!"

BEER-BATTERED CAYENNE GARLIC FRENCH FRIES

These french fries are extra crispy, and have a nice rich flavor thanks to the beer. The cayenne gives the fries a nice kick.

Prep time: 10 minutes
Cook time: 15 minutes
Servings: 4

Ingredients

6 cups peanut oil
6 tbsp. All-purpose flour
½ tsp. Garlic powder
½ tsp. Fine salt, plus more to taste
¾ tsp. Paprika
¼ tsp. Cayenne

¾ cup beer
4 medium-large russet potatoes. Peeled and thinly sliced
Fresh parsley, chopped for garnish

Directions

> Pour the peanut oil in a non-stick skillet and heat on medium heat.
> Mix the dry seasoning ingredients in a bowl using a whisk. Then whisk in the beer.
> Coat the potato slices in batches with the beer batter.
> Shake off any excess batter and use tongs to place the slices in the skillet.
> Fry for 3-4 minutes until the fries turn golden.
> Use the tongs to take the fries out of the skillet and on to a plate that's been lined with paper towels. Repeat the frying process with the remaining fries.
> Pat dry to remove excess oil. Garnish with parsley, and serve.

SOUTHERN FRIED SWEET ONION RINGS

These onion rings have all the flavor of southern fried chicken with just a hint of sweetness.

Prep time: 10 minutes
Cook time: 10 minutes
Servings: 4

Ingredients

6 cups peanut oil
1 ½ cups all-purpose flour
1 ½ cups finely ground cornmeal
½ cup cornstarch
¼ tsp. Cayenne pepper
1 egg

1 cup buttermilk
2 large vidalia or other sweet onions, sliced 1/4-inch thick
Kosher salt

Directions

> Pour the peanut oil in a non-stick skillet and heat on medium heat.
> Mix the cornmeal, cornstarch, flour, and cayenne in a bowl using a whisk. Then whisk in the beer. Use a whisk to beat the buttermilk and egg in a separate bowl. Organize the slices of onion into rings.
> Lightly coat the onion rings with the dry mixture, and then dip them into, the wet mixture, in batches. Then lightly coat the onion rings again with the dry mixture.
> Put the onion rings in your skillet, and cook until they turn golden, about 2-3 minutes. Place the finished onion rings on a paper towel lined plate and let the excess grease drain.
> Pat, salt to taste, and serve.

NONNA'S FRIED SQUASH BLOSSOMS

Squash blossoms are an italian treat that are only available during the late summer. These are packed with flavor from the ricotta filling.

Prep time: 10 minutes
Cook time: 15 minutes
Servings: 4

Ingredients

6 cups peanut oil
1 cup whole-milk ricotta
1 large egg yolk
1/4 cup finely chopped mint
2/3 cup grated parmigiano-reggiano, divided

12 to 16 large zucchini squash blossoms
1/2 cup plus 1 tablespoon all-purpose flour
3/4 cup chilled seltzer or club soda

Directions

> Pour the peanut oil in a non-stick skillet and heat on medium heat.
> In a bowl, mix together the mint, ricotta, egg, 1/3 cup parmigiano, 1/8 teaspoon salt, and 1/8 teaspoon pepper. In a separate bowl, mix together the remaining parmigiano, club soda, flour and ¼ teaspoon salt
> Gently open up the squash blossoms, and carefully spoon in 2 teaspoons of the mint mixture. Then twist the squash blossoms to seal them up.
> Lightly coat the squash blossoms with the flower mixture, in batches.
> Fry the squash blossoms for 1-2 minutes making sure to turn them once while frying. Place the finished squash blossoms on a paper towel lined plate and let the excess grease drain. Salt to taste, and serve.
>

KICKIN CRUNCHY CAJON POPCORN SHRIMP

These shrimp are extra crunchy thanks to the mix of two different kinds of bread crumbs. The cajun seasoning gives the shrimp a great blast of flavor.

Prep time: 1 hour
Cook time: 6 minutes
Servings: 4

Ingredients

6 cups peanut oil
1 (10 ounce, about 40-50 per bag) package of frozen small peeled and deveined prawns, thawed according to package directions
1 tbsp. Cajun seasoning
2 tsp. Olive oil

1/2- 3/4 cup flour
2 eggs
1/3-2/3 cup plain dry bread crumbs
1/3-2/3 cup panko bread crumbs
Kosher salt

Directions

> In a bowl, mix together the olive oil, shrimp, and cajon seasoning. Cover the bowl, and refrigerate it for 1 hour
> While the shrimp is marinating, set out 3 bowls. Place the flour in one, the eggs in another, and the bread crumbs in the third.
> At the end of the marinating time, pour the peanut oil in a non-stick skillet and heat on medium heat.
> Coat the marinated shrimp in the flour, then egg, and then finally the bread crumbs.
> Fry the shrimp in batches, until their golden about 4-6 minutes. Place the finished shrimp on a paper towel lined plate and let the excess grease drain. Fry all the shrimp. And serve.

CRISPY RANCH FRIED PICKLE SPEARS

The panko bread crumbs give these pickles a nice crunchy. The ranch adds a great tangy flavor.

Prep time: 15 minutes
Cook time: 3 minutes
Servings: 4

Ingredients

6 cups peanut oil
2 teaspoons dry ranch dressing mix
1 cup all-purpose flour
4 eggs

12 crisp pickle spears
2 cups panko bread crumbs

Directions

> Pour the peanut oil in a non-stick skillet and heat on medium heat.
> In a bowl, mix together flour and ranch. In a separate bowl, use a whisk to beat the eggs. Place the bread crumbs in a third bowl.
> Coat the pickles with the ranch mixture, then the egg. Coat the pickles with the ranch mixture again, and then the bread crumbs
> Fry the pickles for 2-3 minutes making sure to turn them once while frying, until they're brown. Place the finished pickles on a paper towel lined plate and let the excess grease drain. Serve once they've drained.

5 ALARM CRISPY BUFFALO CHICKEN TENDERS

Combine the best of both worlds with all the fried goodness of chicken tenders, and spicy deliciousness of buffalo sauce. Use the buffalo sauce of your choice.

Prep time: 15 minutes
Cook time: 8 minutes
Servings: 4

Ingredients

6 cups peanut oil
1 lb. Boneless chicken tenders
2 large eggs
1 cup japanese-style bread crumbs or plain dry bread crumbs

2 tbsp. Vegetable oil
1/2 cup frank's redhot® buffalo wings sauce

Directions

> Pour the peanut oil in a non-stick skillet and heat on medium heat.
> Use a whisk to beat the eggs in a bowl. Place the bread crumbs in a separate bowl
> Place the chicken and flour in a resealable plastic bag, seal, and shake until well coated.
> Dip the chicken in the egg, and then the bread crumbs.
> Fry the chicken for 6-8 minutes until golden and cripsy. Place the chicken on a paper towel lined plate and let the excess grease drain. Toss with buffalo sauce, and serve.

PARMESAN CRUNCHY FRIED ZUCCHINI STICKS

These are a great alternative to fries or onion rings. They've got a lovely cheesy flavor, and crunchy texture.

Prep time: 15 minutes
Cook time: 10 minutes
Servings: 4

Ingredients

6 cups peanut oil
1 3/4 cups freshly grated parmesan
1 1/2 cups panko breadcrumbs
3/4 teaspoon salt
2 large eggs

3 medium zucchini, cut into 3-inch long by 1/2-inch wide strips

Directions

> Pour the peanut oil in a non-stick skillet and heat on medium heat.
> Mix together the breadcrumbs, 1 1/2 cup parmesan, and salt in a bowl. Use a whisk to beat the eggs in a separate bowl.
> Dip the zucchini in the egg, and then coat with the parmesan mixture.
> Fry the zucchini until golden and crispy, around 3 minutes. Place the zucchini on a paper towel lined plate and let the excess grease drain. Top with the rest of the parmesan, and serve.

❯

CRUNCHY PARMESAN EGGPLANT BITES

These are almost like bite sized eggplant parmesan. They make a great start to any italian meal.

Prep time: 15 minutes
Cook time: 10 minutes
Servings: 1

Ingredients

6 cups peanut oil
1 small to medium eggplant, cut into 1 inch cubes
3 tbsp. Flour
3 tbsp. Parmesan cheese

2 large eggs
5 tbsp. Breadcrumbs
Salt and pepper

Directions

❯ Pour the peanut oil in a non-stick skillet and heat on medium heat.
❯ Mix together the breadcrumbs and parmesan in a bowl, and salt and pepper to taste. Use a whisk to lightly beat the eggs in a separate bowl. Place the flour in a third bowl
❯ Coat the eggplant with the flour, then dip in the egg, and then coat with the parmesan mixture.
❯ Fry the eggplant in batches until golden and crispy, around 3-4 minutes. Place the eggplant on a paper towel lined plate and let the excess grease drain, and serve.

CRISPY PARMESAN FRIED OKRA

This is a cheesy take on a southern favorite. The parmesan gives the okra a nice saltiness.

Prep time: 15 minutes
Cook time: 4 minutes
Servings: 2

Ingredients

6 cups peanut oil
1 cup sliced <u>fresh okra</u> (slices are about 1/4-inch thick)
1 <u>egg</u>

1/2 cup grated <u>parmesan cheese</u>

Salt and pepper

Directions

> Pour the peanut oil in a non-stick skillet and heat on medium heat.
> Salt and pepper the okra to taste.
> Put the parmesan in a bowl. Use a whisk to beat the eggs in a separate bowl.
> Dip the okra in the egg, and then coat with the parmesan.
> Fry the okra until golden and crispy, around 4 minutes. Place the okra on a paper towel lined plate and let the excess grease drain, and then serve.

CRUNCHY PARMESAN PORTABELLO MUSHROOM FRIES

Think of these as italian mushroom fries. They have a great crunch, cheesy flavor, while remaining soft in the middle.

Prep time: 10 minutes
Cook time: 15 minutes
Servings: 4

Ingredients

6 cups peanut oil
5 large portobello mushrooms
1/2 cup all-purpose flour
1 1/2 cup panko bread crumbs
1/4 cup finely grated parmigiano-reggiano

2 tbsp. Finely chopped fresh parsley leaves
1/2 teaspoon red pepper flakes
salt and freshly ground black pepper
3 eggs, lightly beaten

Directions

> Pour the peanut oil in a non-stick skillet and heat on medium heat.
> Use a knife to remove the gills, and stems from the bottom of the mushrooms. Cut them into ¼ long pieces.
> Put the flour in a bowl. Use a whisk to beat the eggs in a separate bowl. Mix the remaining ingredients in a third bowl.
> Coat the mushrooms in the flour, then eggs, and finally the bread crumb mixture.
> Fry the mushrooms until golden and crispy, around 4 minutes. Place the mushroom on a paper towel lined plate and let the excess grease drain, and then serve.

VEGGIES AND SIDES:

Just like "mom" used to say…"eat your veggies!" Let's break this down for you! Entrée's are amazing, but when you combine the succulent taste of veggies and sides to complete the meal then you have created a masterpiece on the plate. Veggies and sides make the world go round! Just dive in and look at what we have in store for you within these next set of pages. You may find that your kids will also start eating what they would never eat before…and when this happens, you have won the game! Enjoy!

SWEET AND SAVORY POTATO PIZZA

Eggs and sweet potato in a pizza you ask? It can be done and with pizza

Prep time: 20 minutes
Cook time: 20 minutes
Servings: 4

Ingredients

6 eggs
1 cup half-and-half
1 tsp. Kosher salt
½ tsp. Freshly ground pepper
2 cups sweet potatoes

2 cups kale (firmly packed chopped)
½ small red onion
2 cloves garlic
3 oz. Goat cheese

Directions

> Prepare eggs: whisk eggs, salt and pepper and half-and- half in a mixing bowl.
> In a non-stick skillet cook the sweet potatoes for 10 minutes. (lightly oil if desired)
> Transfer to a plate.
> Add the kale, onions and garlic until kale is cooked. Approximately 4 minutes.
> Pour in potatoes and egg mixture for 3 more minutes.
> Add cheese on top showering all over and bake at 345 degrees for 12 minutes.
> Depending on the size of your oven it may take just a couple minutes longer.
> Garnish and serve.

Nutritional Facts:

Serving size 268 g, amount per serving, calories 381, calories from fat 191, total fat 21.2g
Saturated fat 11.6g, trans fat 0.0g, cholesterol 290mg, sodium 794mg, potassium 976mg,
total carbohydrates 29.5g, dietary fiber 3.9g, sugars 1.8g, protein 19.0g

Low in sugar, high in phosphorus, high in selenium, very high in vitamin a, very high in
vitamin c

SQUASH AND GARLIC EGGPLANT LASAGNA–

This recipe will blow you away. Not only are you making lasagna in a skillet, but you are making it without noodles and you won't even be able to tell the difference.

Prep time: 35 minutes
Cook time: 35 minutes
Servings: 6

Ingredients

1 peeled and chopped eggplant
1 chopped zucchini
1 dice yellow squash
3 chopped cloves garlic

1 cup ricotta cheese
3 tbsp. Grated parmesan cheese
1 cup traditional pasta sauce
1 cup shredded mozzarella cheese

Directions

> In a non-stick skillet, add and cook the eggplant, zucchini and squash for 10 minutes.
> Add the garlic and cook for 5 more minutes stirring occasionally. Remove vegetables and keep warm.
> Combine ricotta and parmesan in skillet with pasta sauce.
> Add the cooked vegetable mixture, cover and cook for 20 minutes.
> Let it cool...garnish and serve.

Nutritional Facts:

Serving size 250 g, amount per serving, calories 197, calories from fat 86, total fat 9.6g, saturated fat 5.3g, trans fat 0.0g, cholesterol 29mg, sodium 373mg, potassium 540mg, total carbohydrates 15.8g, dietary fiber 4.5g, sugars 7.3g, protein 13.6g

High in calcium, high in phosphorus, high in vitamin c

CALIFORNIA MEATLESS CILANTRO QUESADILLAS

These easy to make "bursting with flavor" quesadillas take less than 20 minutes to make. This is a perfect recipe for when you want to be healthy but don't have a lot of time to make dinner.

Prep time: 15 minutes
Cook time: 15 minutes
Servings: 4

Ingredients

16oz black beans (can substitute with pinto beans)
½ cup shredded monterey jack cheese
½ cup fresh salsa

4 whole-wheat tortillas (at least 8")
1 ripe diced avocado
¼ cup cilantro

Directions

> Preparing quesadillas: cut up the cilantro very fine!
> Mix the cilantro beans, cheese and salsa in a mixing container.
> Combine mixture into a tortilla, spread evenly and fold. Continue on each until all mixture has been used.
> In a non-stick skillet add two quesadillas and cook for two minutes on both sides. (you will see the tortillas start to brown)
> Repeat.
> Garnish with avocado, and salsa and serve.

Nutritional Facts:

Serving size 235 g, amount per serving, calories 603, calories from fat 148, total fat 16.4g, saturated fat 5.3g, trans fat 0.0g, cholesterol 13mg, sodium 291mg, potassium 2083mg, total carbohydrates 87.9g, dietary fiber 22.7g, sugars 3.9g, protein 30.8g
Very low in cholesterol, low in sodium, low in sugar, high in dietary fiber, high in thiamin

FIRE ROASTED SIZZLING ZUCCHINI AND RICE

Fresh zucchini never tasted soo good! When combined with this rich and healthy dish, these fire roasted tomatoes, beans and rice give you the ultimate flavor for your taste buds in an a simple and easy to cook meal! This flavorful and hearty zucchini dish is a quick prep dish that will make you look like you slaved in the kitchen for hours. This is an amazing dish to impress your peers. They will think you had this dish prepared by a professional chef! Simple, quick and will have your taste buds screaming for more!

Prep time: 25 minutes
Cook time: 25 minutes
Servings: 4

Ingredients

1 chopped zucchini
Tablespoon of butter
½ cup chopped green bell pepper
16 oz black beans (whole 1 can)
14 oz tomatoes (fire roasted)

¾ cup chicken broth
1 cup uncooked instant white rice
½ cup shredded cheese (cheddar and monterey jack cheese blend)

Directions

> In a non-stick skillet heat a tablespoon of butter, then add zucchini and cook for 5 minutes.
> Then add the mixture of beans, tomatoes and water and cook for about 3 min.
> After this starts to boil...add rice, cover and simmer for 7 minutes.
> Garnish with cheese and serve.

Nutritional Facts:

Serving size 288 g, amount per serving, calories 477, calories from fat 72, total fat 8.0g, saturated fat 4.3g, cholesterol 18mg, sodium 216mg, potassium 1703mg, total carbohydrates 77.4g, dietary fiber 15.7g, sugars 5.2g, protein 25.9g
Low in cholesterol, low in sodium, high in dietary fiber, high in thiamin

CHEESEY SPINACH & GARLIC ARTICOKE SKILLET DIP

A little something to dip your chips, veggies, crackers or crusted bread till your hearts content! This one is a sure winner for that pot luck or gathering with friends! This dip is a sure winner and party favorite and will make you look like a pro!

Prep time: 25 minutes
Cook time: 25 minutes
Servings: 4

Ingredients

2 ½ cups fresh baby spinach
3 cloves chopped garlic
1 cup ricotta cheese
1 package cream cheese

1 ½ cups chopped artichoke hearts
1 cup shredded provolone cheese
1 roasted red pepper (garnish)

Directions

> In a non-stick skillet add minced garlic, and baby spinach. Cook for 5 minutes stirring on occasion.
> Turn off heat and stir in cheeses.
> Add the mixture with artichoke hearts and the red pepper to the skillet, with a layer of cheese.
> (you can add a little salt and fresh ground pepper just for flavor)
> Bake for 400 for 6 minutes.
> Garnish with some of the leftover red peppers and serve.
> "great for dipping with buttered with crackers" be creative with what you dip!

Nutritional Facts:

Serving size 204 g, amount per serving, calories 311, calories from fat 192, total fat 21.3g, saturated fat 13.4g, trans fat 0.0g, cholesterol 65mg, sodium 533mg, potassium 470mg, total carbohydrates 12.1g, dietary fiber 3.3g, sugars 1.8g, protein 19.5g

Low in sugar, high in calcium, high in phosphorus, high in vitamin a and vitamin c

MIXED VEGTABLE RELISH–

When you just want vegetables. This mixed vegetable relish will satisfy your hunger cravings in under 30 minutes.

Prep time: 25 minutes
Cook time: 25 minutes
Servings: 10

Ingredients

1 large diced white onion
18 ounces zucchini (chopped medium)
1 large chopped red bell pepper
1 large chopped orange bell pepper
1 10-ounce package frozen lima beans or shelled edamame

1 10-ounce package frozen corn kernels
1 tsp. Minced fresh marjoram
1 tablespoon oregano
Teaspoon fresh ground pepper
1 tsp. Sea salt

Directions -

> In a non-stick skillet combine onions, zucchini, peppers, lima beans and corn and cook for 10 minutes.
> Add marjoram, oregano, sea salt and fresh ground pepper and cook for another 5 minutes.
> Garnish and serve.

Nutritional Facts:

Serving size 157 g, amount per serving, calories 81, calories from fat 6, total fat 0.7g, cholesterol 0mg, sodium 197mg, potassium 434mg, total carbohydrates 16.7g, dietary fiber 3.9g, sugars 4.2g, protein 3.8g

Very low in saturated fat, no cholesterol, high in dietary fiber, high in iron, very high in manganese, high in magnesium, high in phosphorus, high in potassium, very high in vitamin a, very high in vitamin b6, very high in vitamin c

THE TASTE OF SPRING IN A SKILLET

Spring is in the air and what better way to celebrate the season then by adding it to your plate. This is a recipe that brings all of the beauty of spring right into your kitchen.

Prep time: 15 minutes
Cook time: 15 minutes
Servings: 4

Ingredients

16 baby carrots (peeled and chopped with tops)
¾ tsp. Kosher salt
12 ounces sugar snap peas

1 tbsp. Chopped fresh tarragon
¼ tbsp. Freshly ground black pepper
1 tbsp. Grated lemon rind
1 tsp. Fresh lemon juice

Directions -

> Prepare vegetables: cut all vegetables to your liking.
> Bring water, carrots and peas to a boil in a non-stick saucepan for only a few minutes until soft but firm. Then disregard water.
> In a non-stick skillet combine vegetables, seasoning, rind and lemon juice, cook for 2 minutes.

Nutritional Facts:

Serving size 132 g, amount per serving, calories 53, calories from fat 3, total fat 0.3g, cholesterol 0mg, sodium 473mg, potassium 290mg, total carbohydrates 10.5g, dietary fiber 3.6g, sugars 5.4g, protein 2.8g

Very low in saturated fat, no cholesterol, high in calcium, very high in dietary fiber, very high in iron, very high in manganese, high in magnesium, high in pantothenic acid, high in phosphorus, high in potassium, high in thiamin, very high in vitamin a, high in vitamin b6 Very high in vitamin c

COATED ASPARAGUS WITH RIPE AVACADO

Asparagus and avocado are great additions to any meal, so why not put them together in the same dish? There is no reason not to outside of an allergy of course. Plenty of other vegetables make this a colorful salad full of freshness and flavor!

Prep time: 20 minutes
Cook time: 23 minutes
Servings: 4

Ingredients

1 1/2 pounds fresh asparagus
1/2 cup olive oil, divided
1 1/2 tablespoons chopped fresh basil, divided
1/2 teaspoon lemon pepper
1/2 teaspoon salt, divided
1/4 cup balsamic vinegar
1 garlic clove, minced

1 cup halved cherry tomatoes (about 1/2 pt.)
1/2 cup chopped red bell pepper
1/8 cup finely chopped red onion
1/8 cup finely chopped sweet yellow onion
1 head bibb lettuce, torn into bite-size pieces
1 avocado, sliced
Parsley for garnish

Directions

> Turn oven on to 450° to preheat for cooking. Cut off the ends of asparagus and dispose of.
> In a mixing container, add 1 tbsp. Olive oil, 1 ½ teaspoon basil, lemon pepper, and 1/4 tsp. Salt.
> Get a brush & coat (lightly brush) asparagus with olive oil mixture, and place on sheet.
> Bake for 10 to 12 minutes, then let the asparagus sit and cool for 8-10 minutes.
> Take the balsamic vinegar, garlic, and remaining olive oil, basil, and salt...stirring and mixing it all together.
> Combine tomatoes, bell pepper, onion, and 1 tbsp. Balsamic vinegar mixture and toss.
> Put the tomato mixture and asparagus over some lettuce on each plate, slice an avocado and divide, an with a brush...brush the rest of the balsamic mix to your liking.

Nutritional Facts:

Serving size 410 g, amount per serving, calories 383, calories from fat 319, total fat 35.5g, saturated fat 5.7g, trans fat 0.0g, cholesterol 0mg, sodium 306mg, potassium 863mg, total carbohydrates 17.1g, dietary fiber 8.5g, sugars 6.3g, protein 5.8g

No cholesterol, high in vitamin a, high in vitamin b6, high in vitamin c

SIMMERING BARLEY PARMESEAN

Barley is one of the healthiest side dishes because it contains protein, fiber, and is considered a whole grain. In addition, it is not short on flavor! The barley mixes well with the tomatoes and cheese providing a side dish that is gratifying enough to be its own meal. Beer is still an option as a side to this side.

Prep time: 10 minutes
Cook time: 30 minutes
Servings: 4

Ingredients

2 tablespoons olive oil
1 onion, finely chopped
1/2 teaspoon salt
1/4 teaspoon pepper
2 cups quick-cook barley
1 can (28 oz.) Diced tomatoes, drained
1 cup dry white wine

2 1/2 cups water
8 cups mustard green leaves or spinach, torn into pieces
2 ounces brie (rind removed), cut into small pieces
1/2 cup grated parmesan (2 oz.)
1/4 cup chopped oregano

Directions

> Add oil to a pan over medium heat. Cook the onion with salt and pepper, and stir occasionally for 5-7 minutes.
> Mix in the barley, tomatoes, wine and water and increase heat, bringing the ingredients to a simmering boil.
> Lower the heat keeping the simmer for 10-12 minutes while continuing to stir the barley in the pan.
> Mix in the mustard greens, brie, oregano, and ¼ cup of the cheese and cook an additional several minutes while stirring making it nice and creamy.
> Divide and shower the servings with what is left of the parmesan.
> Delicious…

Nutritional Facts:

Serving size 612 g, amount per serving, calories 566, calories from fat 134, total fat 14.9g, saturated fat 4.6g, trans fat 0.0g, cholesterol 15mg, sodium 456mg, potassium 1412mg, total carbohydrates 84.8g, dietary fiber 22.2g, sugars 8.1g, protein 19.3g

Low in cholesterol, high in dietary fiber, high in manganese, high in selenium, very high in vitamin a, high in vitamin c

FRESH AND FLAVORFUL CAPRESE PASTA

A vegetarian's delight! This caprese pasta salad is light and fresh and will add flavor to any main course. It's quick, easy, and satisfying. There's nothing more you can really ask for. The tomatoes and mozzarella mixed with the basil offers a true italian taste wherever you're dining.

Prep time: 5 minutes
Cook time: 10 minutes
Servings: 4

Ingredients

6 ounces whole grain fusilli or rotini pasta
⅓ cup olive oil
2 cloves minced garlic
2 pints cherry or grape tomatoes
½ teaspoon sea salt

8 ounces baby mozzarella balls (ciliegine)
2 tablespoons chopped basil
2 tablespoons chopped oregano
2 to 3 teaspoons white balsamic vinegar, to taste

Directions

> Boil the pasta in a large pot of water (always add a little salt to boil faster and for a little flavor), drain, then use the same pot to set aside the pasta.
> Meanwhile, add olive oil to a large pot or pan over low to medium heat. (do not cook the olive oil on too high because it can burn at high temperatures) cook the tomatoes, garlic, and ½ teaspoon sea salt with the cover on. Make sure to check occasionally but keep mixing anywhere from 6-7 minutes. Pour everything into the pasta and mix it all in nicely.
> Slice the mozzarella balls in half and add to the mixture along with oregano and basil. The vinegar can be added but make sure you add just a little for flavoring. (vinegar can be pretty strong so add moderately)

Nutritional Facts:

Serving size 224 g, amount per serving, calories 368, calories from fat 104, total fat 11.6g. Saturated fat 6.3g, trans fat 0.0g, cholesterol 61mg, sodium 590mg, potassium 385mg, total carbohydrates 46.0g, dietary fiber 3.5g, sugars 15.1g, protein 22.6g

High in calcium, high in phosphorus

POTENT STUFFED PARMESAN PORTEBELLO GRATIN

The beauty of mushrooms is that they can be cooked in different ways, cooked with different things, and serve as a side to most dishes. A very useful vegetable! With this being said, of course bread crumbs and cheese would go well with mushrooms. Add herbs to the filling and you have a deliciously awesome dish.

Prep time: 15 minutes
Cook time: 35 minutes
Servings: 6

Ingredients

2 tablespoons olive oil, plus more for baking sheet
6 portobello mushrooms, stems removed and reserved
1/4 cup finely grated parmesan cheese (1 ounce)
1/4 cup plain dry breadcrumbs
3 tablespoons finely chopped fresh flat-leaf parsley

3 tablespoons chopped fresh chives
2 shallots, thinly sliced
1 pound white or cremini mushrooms, sliced
1/2 cup dry white wine
1/2 cup heavy cream
1 teaspoon coarse salt
1/4 teaspoon freshly ground pepper
1/4 teaspoon red pepper flakes

Directions

> Preheat oven to 350 degrees to get it ready for the mushrooms. Place the portobello caps with their gill sides down and lightly brush oil in the bottom of the skillet. Cook in the oven for about 20 minutes then let cool. (the mushrooms should be pretty tender by this time)
> Turn on the broiler.
> In a mixing container, mix together cheese, breadcrumbs, 1 tablespoon parsley, 1 tablespoon chives, and 1 tablespoon oil.
> Dice up the mushroom stems. Add the remaining oil to a skillet and cook these over medium to low heat. Cook the shallots and make sure you keep mixing while cooking for 2-4 minutes then mix in the mushrooms and the diced stems, cooking and mixing for

133

an additional 5 minutes. The wine can then be added, and then after 2 more minutes and stir in cream. The remainder of both the parsley and chives, and the salt and red and black pepper. After everything is combined, turn off the heat and remove the pan from the burner. (doing this keeps the dish from cooking too long)

> Place the mushroom caps on a clean baking sheet with their gills facing up. Evenly spread the mixture and crumbs atop each cap. Broil for 2 minutes. (you will notice them getting a nice crisp brown...then they're done!) Fast...fun dish for everyone to enjoy!

Nutritional Facts:

Serving size 227 g, amount per serving, calories 240, calories from fat 140, total fat 15.5g. Saturated fat 6.0g, cholesterol 28mg, sodium 592mg, potassium 728mg, total carbohydrates 14.5g, dietary fiber 1.5g, sugars 3.2g, protein 7.2g

High in niacin, high in riboflavin, very high in selenium, very high in vitamin b6

SAUTEED VEGGIES ATOP A BED OF SPICY QUINOA

Kee-noo-ah. The name isn't why the grain is great, but is the most complex part of this side dish. Quinoa is a very healthy alternative to already-healthy foods like rice, and is gradually becoming part of the superfood category. The black beans, spices, and corn give the grain a mexican kick in this sure-to-please healthy side dish!

Prep time: 15 minutes
Cook time: 35 minutes
Servings: 6

Ingredients

1 teaspoon ground cumin
1 1/2 cups vegetable broth
3/4 cup quinoa
3 cloves garlic, chopped
1 onion, chopped
1 teaspoon vegetable oil
1/2 cup chopped fresh cilantro

2 (15 ounce) cans black beans, rinsed and drained
1 cup frozen corn kernels
Salt and ground black pepper to taste
1/4 teaspoon cayenne pepper
1/4 teaspoon paprika
1/4 teaspoon basil

Directions

> Add oil to a saucepan over medium heat and cook the onion and garlic for about 7-8 minutes while occasionally stirring.
> Place quinoa into the onions and garlic, smothering the mixture with vegetable broth. Sprinkle the seasonings, with the exception of the cilantro and bring everything to a boil. Lower the heat and cover the pan, letting the ingredients cook for approximate 15-18 minutes.
> While it remains simmering, pour in the corn and cook for about 5 minutes. Lastly, add the cilantro and black beans.
> If you've never had quinoa...you will be a believer of this dish! :)

Nutritional Facts:

Serving size 274 g, amount per serving, calories 613, calories from fat 43, total fat 4.7g, saturated fat 1.0g, cholesterol 0mg, sodium 589mg, potassium 2391mg, total carbohydrates 110.3g, dietary fiber 24.3g, sugars 4.9g, protein 36.0g

Low in saturated fat, no cholesterol, low in sugar, high in dietary fiber, high in magnesium, very high in phosphorus

5 BEAN LEMON AND GARLIC DRESSING SALAD

Beans are a great source of protein, and you will need it during the backyard games of your summer party. Beans are also very versatile and flavorful, especially considering there are many to choose from. This side dish is the best example for there are 5 included! This hearty course will be a perfect complement for a cookout.

Prep time: 15 minutes
Cook time: 25 minutes
Servings: 6

Ingredients

1/4 c. Olive oil
1/4 c. Fresh lemon juice
Zest of 1 lemon
1 shallot finely chopped
1 garlic clove, finely minced
1 tbsp. Chopped fresh thyme
Kosher salt
Freshly ground black pepper

1 1/2 c. Fresh lima beans
1 c. Fresh black-eyed peas
1/2 lb. Smoked ham hock
1 c. Fresh lady peas
1/2 lb. Yellow wax beans
1/2 lb. Sugar snap peas
1/2 c. Chopped almonds
1/4 c. Chopped cilantro

Directions

›   In a mixing container, add oil, lemon juice, garlic, shallot, and thyme. Add salt and pepper to season after it has been whisked.

›   In your medium pan, cover and simmer lima beans, black-eyed peas, and ham hock in water for 15-18 minutes. Add lady peas and continue to cook at the same heat for 8-10 minutes. Before draining, take out the ham hock and then cool by running the beans under cold water.

›   Bring salted water to a boil in a medium sized pan and cook wax beans and sugar snaps for just a few minutes. Drain all of the water out, then to cool run these under cool water as well.

›   Add everything together and apply the dressing and toss until all ingredients are coated very nicely!

> This is a hearty mouth-watering meal to smile over! ;)

Nutritional Facts:

Serving size 255 g, amount per serving, calories 338, calories from fat 168, total fat 18.7g Saturated fat 3.7g, trans fat 0.0g, cholesterol 36mg, sodium 194mg, potassium 630mg, total carbohydrates 24.5g, dietary fiber 7.5g, sugars 4.8g, protein 20.3g

High in thiamin, very high in vitamin c

JOLLY GREEN BEANS AND SHALLOTS WITH SIZZLING BACON

Even a specific giant would appreciate this flavorful side dish, especially considering bacon is added. However, the meat is not the reason this course is so delightful; you must give the shallots and blue cheese credit as well. This could be a definite addition to the thanksgiving menu, but also accepted year round!

Prep time: **25 minutes**
Cook time: 15 minutes
Servings: 4

Ingredients

1 lb. Fresh green beans, trimmed
4 slices bacon
2 shallots, sliced
4 cloves minced garlic

¼ teaspoon salt
¼ teaspoon freshly ground black pepper
1/8 teaspoon ground red pepper (cayenne)
1/3 cup crumbled blue cheese

Directions

> Bring 2 quarts of water to a boil in a saucepan. Cook the green beans for 5 minutes, covered. Fill a pot of ice water, take the beans off the heat and the immediately place them in the water . When they are finally cold then you can drain them.
> While the beans are cooking, cook the bacon until crisp in a skillet; place the bacon on something that will absorb the grease to drain then crumble the bacon after it's dry. Make sure you keep just a little bit of the bacon grease in skillet. (for flavor of course)
> Using the bacon drippings, cook the shallots over medium heat, turning and mixing while cooking. Mix in the green beans, and season with black and red pepper and salt and cook for just a few minutes while occasionally stirring. (just enough to heat up the dish)
> Top the bean mixture with cheese and bacon crumbles before serving this delicious delight...yum! ;)

Nutritional Facts:

Serving size 171 g, amount per serving, calories 243, calories from fat 137, total fat 15.2gm, saturated fat 6.0gm, trans fat 0.0gm, cholesterol 40mgm, sodium 968mgm, potassium 488mgm, total carbohydrates 12.2gm, dietary fiber 4.0g, sugars 1.7g, protein 15.5g

Low in sugar, high in phosphorus, high in selenium, high in vitamin c,

MOUNTAINOUS BUTTERMILK MASHED POTATOES

Every cook, beginner or experienced, needs at least one mashed potato recipe, so you might as well go all out with it! Butter, milk, buttermilk for good measure, and of course yukon gold potatoes make this heavy side dish a force to be reckon with, but too tempting to resist. It would be wise to serve in moderation so there are leftovers for yourself.

Prep time: 15 minutes
Cook time: 35 minutes
Servings: 8

Ingredients

3/4 cup butter
4 pounds yukon gold potatoes, peeled and
cut into 2-inch pieces
1 tablespoon salt, divided
3/4 cup buttermilk

1/2 cup milk
1/4 teaspoon pepper
Garnishes: fresh parsley, rosemary, and
thyme sprigs
1/4 cup chives

Directions

> Melt butter in a large saucepan to melt the butter, frequently stirring over medium heat. Pour all but 1-2 tbsp. Into a small container and reserve the remainder.

> In a large pot, cover and boil potatoes, water and a few pinches of salt for 15-18 minutes. Drain and then return potatoes to the pot, and cook and a reduced heat for 3-5 minutes, make sure to mix the potatos while cooking. At this point the potatos should be dry.

> Using a potato masher, soften the potatoes as desired. (if you do not have a potato masher just use something that will mash up the potatos) mix all together the rest of the butter from the bowl, buttermilk, milk, pepper, chives, and the rest of the salt.

> Trickle the reserved butter over the potatoes after transferring them to a serving dish.

> Use more butter for a more buttery flavor if desired!

Nutritional Facts:

Serving size 301 g, amount per serving, calories 361, calories from fat 170, total fat 18.9g, saturated fat 11.7, cholesterol 48mg, sodium 1054mg, potassium 1086mg, total carbohydrates 46.6g, dietary fiber 6.1g, sugars 3.4g, protein 6.7g

High in iron, very high in vitamin c

PAN-FRIED OKRA WITH CHICKEN BOUILLON

This side is a charming southern-style stir-fry. The beauty of the dish is that it is pan-fried instead of deep-fried, leaving it healthier without sacrificing flavor! The tomatoes and lime add freshness to the okra that bodes well with the summer air. A light and tasty side dish for any barbeque.

Prep time: 15 minutes
Cook time: 6 minutes
Servings: 4

Ingredients

2 pounds fresh okra
1/2 cup vegetable oil
1 medium-size red onion, thinly sliced
4 cloves minced garlic
2 large tomatoes, seeded

2 tablespoons lime juice
1 1/2 teaspoons salt
1 1/2 teaspoons pepper
1 teaspoon chicken bouillon granules

Directions

> Slice lengthwise to halve the okra.
> Cook okra for 6 minutes in 1/4 cup oil into a large skillet over medium-high. Turn each of the okra frequently and cook in clusters if needed. Drain the vegetable in a colander (paper towels usually work best) until dry and let cool.
> In a large mixing container, combine the remaining ingredients; toss in the okra and coat. Serve.

Nutritional Facts:

Serving size 359 g, amount per serving, calories 356, calories from fat 252, total fat 28.0g Saturated fat 5.5g, cholesterol 0mg, sodium 902mg, potassium 926mg, total carbohydrates 22.1g, dietary fiber 8.7g, sugars 6.0g, protein 5.5g

No cholesterol, high in manganese, high in vitamin a, very high in vitamin c

SWEET ORANGE & GINGER BRUSSEL SPROUTS

Brussels sprouts: ick! That is always the general consensus, but the dish is misunderstood. How could they be gross with orange and ginger glazed over them? They can't be! This flavorful side will give your diners a different opinion about brussels sprouts and keep them wanting more.

Prep time: 10 minutes
Cook time: 5 minutes
Servings: 2

Ingredients

10 to 12 brussels sprouts
1 tablespoon butter
1 teaspoon grated orange rind
1/4 cup freshly squeezed orange juice

1/4 teaspoon ground ginger
2 tablespoons chopped fresh parsley
1/2 teaspoon cornstarch
1 tablespoon thyme

Directions

> Wash and trim brussels sprouts.
> Have the sprouts and then steam them for 5 minutes. Drain and set aside. (you can boil if desired)
> Add the brussels sprouts and ground ginger to melted butter in a skillet then season with thyme, salt, and pepper.
> Pour in orange juice and add the cornstarch and cook for about 3 minutes, mixing them until the sauce begins to become richen and thick.
> Garnish with parsley after transferring to a dish where you will serve them.

Nutritional Facts:

 serving size 140 g, amount per serving, calories 115, calories from fat 57, total fat 6.3g, saturated fat 3.8g, cholesterol 15mg, sodium 68mg, potassium 470mg, total carbohydrates 14.0g, dietary fiber 4.4g, sugars 4.7g, protein 3.8g

CREAMY PEARLED ONION SPINACH WITH AND BACON

Pearl onions are an elegant addition to most meals, and a way to contain the flavor of one of the most used vegetables. They complement well with spinach and cream, and bacon once again offers its unique essence to the course. The best of all worlds are mixed together in this side!

Prep time: 10 minutes
Cook time: 30 minutes
Servings: 4

Ingredients
1 1/4 pounds spinach
10 ounces white pearl onions (about 2 1/2 cups)
6 cloves minced garlic
5 tablespoons unsalted butter
2 tablespoons all-purpose flour
1 1/4 cups milk

3 ounces slab bacon, cut into 1/4-inch dice (about 3/4 cups)
Coarse salt and freshly ground pepper
Generous pinch of freshly grated nutmeg
1/2 cup heavy cream
2 teaspoons lemon juice

Directions
> Cook washed spinach, covered in a large pot over medium heat, for 1 minute. Stir, recover, and cook for an additional minute. Remove the cover and stir until leaves are wilted or turning cooked.
> Rinse spinach under cold water using a colander. Pat dry with paper towel (kitchen towel works as well) then chop to make the spinach finely cut up.
> Boil onions and garlic in water for 3-4 minutes in a saucepan. Save the water in the pot after removing onions and garlic; rinse them with cold water and trim the onions after rinsing them.
> Place the onions back into water that was cooking and cook for 10-12 minutes. After draining, rinse in cold water again.
> Whisk together flour and melted butter in a saucepan over medium heat until smooth. While whisking, slowly add milk and boil for one minute then remove from the heat.

> Using a different saucepan, melt the rest of the butter on low to medium heat. Cook bacon for 6 minutes then add onions and spinach. Pour in the mixture with the milk and the cream. Continue to cook, adding 1/4 teaspoon pepper, 1 teaspoon salt, and nutmeg while continuing to stir frequently for 10 more minutes, but avoid bringing to a boil. Add the lemon juice and a pinch of salt and pepper to your liking.

Nutritional Facts:

Serving size 356 g, amount per serving, calories 416, calories from fat 280, total fat 31.1g, saturated fat 16.6g, trans fat 0.0g, cholesterol 88mg, sodium 1333mg, potassium 1106mg, total carbohydrates 21.1g, dietary fiber 5.0g, sugars 7.2g, protein 16.4g

High in manganese, very high in vitamin a, high in vitamin b6, high in vitamin c

BUTTERY POTATOES TOSSED WITH PARSLEY

Sometimes appearance can go a long way, and when it comes to cooking, it is worth it, and it's simple! These boiled potatoes are a delicious hearty meal, but chopped parsley mixed in provides a great sight and a great taste with little work involved.

Prep time: 10 minutes
Cook time: 20 minutes
Servings: 4

Ingredients

2 pounds small red potatoes
2 teaspoons coarse salt
2 tablespoons unsalted butter

2 tablespoons roughly chopped fresh flat-leaf parsley
1/4 cup chopped green onions
Freshly ground pepper

Directions

> For each potato, peel the middle.
> Cover the potatoes with cold water in a large saucepan and bring to a boil. Reduce the heat to medium and cook for 20 minutes or until potatos are soft in the center.
> Use a colander to drain them, then put them back into the pan while it's still warm. Add the butter, green onions, and parsley and toss it all together, then season with ground pepper. Serve while still warm.

Nutritional Facts:

Serving size 252 g, amount per serving, calories 230, calories from fat 57, total fat 6.3g, saturated fat 3.8g, cholesterol 15mg, sodium 1020mg, potassium 1151mg, total carbohydrates 41.2g, dietary fiber 6.0g, sugars 2.5g, protein 5.3g

Low in cholesterol, high in dietary fiber, high in manganese, high in potassium, high in vitamin c

REFRESHING VEGGIE & HERB RATATOUILLE

There is no need for the assistance of a cartoon rat to cook this easy side dish, you just need plenty of vegetables and you're set! The zucchini and eggplant give the meal plenty of substance and the spices and flavorings bring it all together. Mix everything into a sauté pan and enjoy!

Prep time: 30 minutes
Cook time: 30 minutes
Servings: 4

Ingredients

1 tbsp. Olive oil
1 medium sized red onion, peeled and diced
3 cloves of garlic, chopped
1 red bell pepper, seeded and diced
1 medium italian eggplant, diced
2 tomatoes, seeded and diced
1 zucchini, trimmed and diced

Salt and freshly ground pepper
Juice of 1/2 a lemon
2 tbsp. Fresh basil, chopped
2 tbsp. Chopped oregano
Extra-virgin olive oil to taste
Several leaves of basil, chiffonade

Directions

> Add olive oil in a large sauté pan over medium-high heat.
> Sauté and mix onions for 2 minutes in oil, adding the garlic after and cooking for an additional minute.
> Sauté the red pepper and eggplant for 3-5 minutes, being mindful of the heat because you do not want the vegetables to burn.
> Cook the tomato and zucchini and season with salt (just for a little flavor.) Add pepper and squeeze in lemon juice. The zucchini should be ready when it's tender.
> After mixing in the oregano and basil quickly take it off of the heat.
> Garnish with basil and sprinkle a light amount of olive oil over the dish.

Nutritional Facts:

Serving size 281 g, amount per serving, calories 105, calories from fat 40, total fat 4.5g, saturated fat 0.7g, cholesterol 0mg, sodium 595mg, potassium 678mg, total carbohydrates 16.2g, dietary fiber 7.4g, sugars 7.8g, protein 3.2g

No cholesterol, very high in dietary fiber, high in iron, very high in manganese, high in magnesium, high in potassium, very high in vitamin a, high in vitamin b6, very high in vitamin c

SWEET & SIMPLE GARLIC SEARED ASPARAGUS

There won't be an easier dish to make that provides this much flavor from basic ingredients. Asparagus goes well with most main courses, so having the vegetable as a side is always a smart decision. Garlic, asparagus, salt and pepper, and enjoy! It's that simple.

Prep time: 5 minutes
Cook time: 15 minutes
Servings: 4

Ingredients

1 pound fresh asparagus spears, trimmed
3 cloves garlic, minced
1/4 teaspoon ground black pepper
1 teaspoon coarse salt

1 teaspoon red pepper flakes
1 teaspoon cayenne
2 tablespoons olive oil
1/4 cup butter

Directions

> Season asparagus with red pepper and cayenne.
> In a skillet over medium high heat add butter. Once melted, mix in olive oil and salt and pepper. First cook the garlic for a minute, adding the asparagus afterwards and continuing to cook for an additional 8-10 minutes, turning occasionally to verify they have cooked evenly.
> Delicious and simple...tasty meal packed with vitamins! Delicious! ;)

Nutrition facts:

Serving size 140 g, amount per serving, calories 191, calories from fat 169, total fat 18.8g, saturated fat 8.4g. Cholesterol 31mg. Sodium 565mg. Potassium 261mg. Total carbohydrates 5.7g, dietary fiber 2.7g, sugars 2.3g, protein 2.9g

High in vitamin a

VEGGIE BOATS FOR MEAT SAILORS

Your parents told you never to play with your food, but then offered you "ants on a log." This is the adult version; instead of celery you have zucchini, and instead of raisins and peanut butter you have beef and cheese! Go ahead & play with your food, you've earned it.

Prep time: 10 minutes
Cook time: 10 minutes
Servings: 4

Ingredients

4 medium zucchini, halved and scooped
1 tablespoon olive oil
1/2 white onion, diced
2 cloves minced garlic
1 jalapeño pepper, seeded and diced
1 pound ground beef

1 teaspoon ground cumin
1/2 cup salsa
1 cup grated cheddar cheese
Salt and pepper
Fresh cilantro, to garnish

Directions

> Cut the zucchini and scoop out seeds. Make sure to halve long ways.
> Add olive oil to a skillet over medium-high heat. Cook the onions, garlic, and peppers for 3-4 minutes, just enough to soften in the pan. Sprinkle a few pinches of salt and pepper each to season.
> Next, season the ground beef with cumin and place in the pan. You will cook this in with the vegetables. After the beef has browned, pour in salsa and stir until everything is combined.
> Mix in the cheddar cheese after removing the skillet from the heat.
> Make sure each zucchini receives the same amount of beef filling and then grill the boats for 5 or 6 minutes. Make sure that the zucchini does not get to be too soft and fragile.
> You may use cilantro to garnish and also dust cheese over the top. Make sure it's warm when served.

Nutritional Facts:

Serving size 406 g, amount per serving, calories 410, calories from fat 185, total fat 20.6g, saturated fat 9.2g, cholesterol 131mg, sodium 1051mg, potassium 1189mg, total carbohydrates 12.0g, dietary fiber 3.6g1, sugars 5.5g, protein 45.0g

Very high in iron, high in phosphorus, high in selenium, very high in vitamin b6, very high in vitamin b12, high in vitamin c, high in zinc

FRESH AND VIGOROUS VEGGIE PASTA

For all the vegetarians out there, this pasta is a perfect dish, and don't worry, carnivores, it's okay to take a break from the meat once in a while, you're allowed to! Fresh zucchini and peppers sautéed and served with mozzarella over pasta seems simple enough and it is. The dish is light, but enough will leave you full and satisfied no matter your food preference.

Prep time: 10 minutes
Cook time: 20 minutes
Servings: 4

Ingredients

2 tbsp. Unsalted butter
1 tbsp. Extra-virgin olive oil
3 small bell peppers, orange, yellow, and red, thinly sliced
1 small onion, thinly sliced
4 cloves garlic, minced
Kosher salt
Freshly ground black pepper

2 medium zucchini, cut into 1/2"-thick slices
12 oz. Fettuccine pasta
4 oz. Smoked mozzarella, grated (about 1 cup) + more for serving
1/8 c. Fresh basil, torn
1/8 c. Fresh oregano, torn

Directions

> Using the package directions, cook pasta. Keep at least a cup of the water from the pasta and drain the rest from the pasta.
> Meanwhile...combine butter and oil, peppers, garlic, and onion, along with salt and pepper seasoning in your skillet and cook over medium heat. Make sure you cook for at least 10 minutes, stirring occasionally. Lastly, cook the zucchini for 4-6 minutes, stirring in the flavor.
> Season the pepper mixture with basil, oregano, salt and pepper, then add the pasta, mozzarella, and ½ cup of the reserved pasta water. Keep tossing the mixture until it is all coated with the sauce mixture.
> Sprinkle the dish with more mozzarella, fresh basil and oregano if desired.

Nutritional Facts:

Serving size 301 g, amount per serving, calories 492, calories from fat 191, total fat 21.2g, saturated fat 10.5g, cholesterol 107mg, sodium 291mg, potassium 633mg, total carbohydrates 57.6g, dietary fiber 3.7g, sugars 5.0g, protein 19.1g

High in vitamin a, very high in vitamin c

LEMON GARLIC STEAMED BROCCOLI

Looking for a healthy sides, but bored with the flavor of steamed vegetables? The citrus flavor of the lemon, and aromatic flavor of the garlic kick this steamed broccoli up a notch.

Prep time: 10 minutes
Cook time: 5 minutes
Servings: 2

Ingredients

2 cups water
1 small bunch broccoli (about 3/4 pound)
1 garlic clove, finely chopped
1 1/2 tablespoons olive oil

1 1/2 teaspoons fresh lemon juice
Salt
Freshly ground black pepper

Directions

> Cut the leaves off the broccoli, and cut the broccoli into florets
> Place the water in your skillet, and place the steamer tray in your skillet. Bring the water to a boil, and place the broccoli on the steamer tray. Place the lid on the skillet, and steam for 4-5 minutes.
> During the steaming process place the garlic lemon, and olive oil in a small pan. Heat on medium heat until garlic becomes fragrant. Salt and pepper to taste.
> Mix the steamed broccoli with the oil mixture, and serve.

SPICY HARISSA STEAMED CAULIFLOWER

Harissa is a spicy middle eastern pepper sauce that any spicy food fan will love. The sauce gives the mild cauliflower a bold flavor.

Prep time: 5 minutes
Cook time: 5 minutes
Servings: 2

Ingredients
2 cups water
1 small bunch broccoli (about 3/4 pound)
2 teaspoons harissa

Salt
Freshly ground black pepper

Directions
> Cut the leaves off the cauliflower, and cut the cauliflower into florets
> Place the water in your skillet, and place the steamer tray in your skillet. Bring the water to a boil, and place the cauliflower on the steamer tray. Place the lid on the skillet, and steam for 4-5 minutes.
> Mix the steamed broccoli with the harissa, salt and pepper to taste, and serve.

SAVORY DIJON GARLIC STEAMED VEGETABLES

This is great, easy dish to make. Simply use whatever vegetables you have on hand. The dijon garlic sauce gives the vegetables a delicious savory flavor.

Prep time: 5 minutes
Cook time: 5 minutes
Servings: 4

Ingredients

2 cups water
1 lb. Vegetables of your choice
1 tbsp. Whole grain dijon mustard
2 tsp. White balsamic vinegar
2½ tbsp. Extra-virgin olive oil

Salt
Freshly ground black pepper
½ clove garlic (crushed)

Directions

> Slice your vegetables if necessary.
> Place the water in your skillet, and place the steamer tray in your skillet. Bring the water to a boil, and place the vegetables on the steamer tray. Place the lid on the skillet, and steam for 4-5 minutes.
> Place the remaining ingredients in a jar, and shake it until the ingredients are well mixed.
> Mix the steamed broccoli with the dijon sauce, salt and pepper to taste, and serve.
>

ZESTY LEMON PESTO BROCCOLINI

Although it might look like broccoli, broccolini is a completely different flavor. It has a sweet flavor, and goes well with both the pesto and lemon.

Prep time: 5 minutes
Cook time: 5 minutes
Servings: 6

Ingredients

2 cups water
1 lb. Broccolini
2 teaspoons fresh lemon juice

Salt
Freshly ground black pepper
1 tbsp. Pesto sauce

Directions

> Wash and trim the broccolini.
> Place the water in your skillet, and place the steamer tray in your skillet. Bring the water to a boil, and place the broccolini on the steamer tray. Place the lid on the skillet, and steam for 5 minutes.
> Toss the steamed broccolini with the pesto and lemon juice, salt and pepper to taste, and serve.

SPICY AND SAVORY MISO-GINGER STEAMED ASPARAGUS

This isn't your average steamed asparagus. The miso gives it a savory flavor, while the ginger gives it a spicy aromatic kick.

Prep time: 10 minutes
Cook time: 5 minutes
Servings: 4

Ingredients

2 cups water
1 lb. Asparagus
1 tsp. Brown rice vinegar
1 tsp. Mirin
½ tsp. Finely grated ginger

2 tbsps. Olive oil
1 tbsp. Water
Salt
Freshly ground black pepper
1 tbsp. White miso

Directions

> Cut the woody bottoms off the bottom of the asparagus.
> Place the 2 cups water in your skillet, and place the steamer tray in your skillet. Bring the water to a boil, and place the asparagus on the steamer tray. Place the lid on the skillet, and steam for 5 minutes.
> While the asparagus is steaming, mix together the miso and 1 tablespoon water until they become smooth. Then mix in the ginger, vinegar, and mirin. Slowly whisk in the olive oil.
> Toss the steamed asparagus with the ginger-miso sauce, salt and pepper to taste, and serve.
>

SPICY CHILI LIME BRUSSEL SPROUTS

This will completely change the way you look at brussel sprouts. The chili lime butter gives bitter brussel sprouts a sweet, citrusy flavor that packs a kick.

Prep time: 5 minutes
Cook time: 5 minutes
Servings: 4

Ingredients

2 cups water
1 lb. Brussel sprouts
2 tbsps. Butter
½ tsp. Salt
1 tsp. Grated lime peel

1 garlic clove, finely chopped
1 tsp. Finely chopped serrano or jalapeño chile
1 tbsp. Fresh lime juice

Directions

> Cut the bottoms off the brussel sprouts, and then cut them in half.
> Place the water in your skillet, and place the steamer tray in your skillet. Bring the water to a boil, and place the brussel sprouts on the steamer tray. Place the lid on the skillet, and steam for 5 minutes.
> While the brussel sprouts are steaming, put the butter in a small pan, and melt it on low heat. Put in the garlic, allow it to cook for 20-30 seconds, mix in the remaining ingredients, and set aside.
> Toss the steamed brussel sprouts with the chili lime butter, salt and pepper to taste if necessary, and serve.
>

BALSAMIC VINAIGRETTE STEAMED EGGPLANT

This will completely change the way you look at brussel sprouts. The chili lime butter gives bitter brussel sprouts a sweet, citrusy flavor that packs a kick.

Prep time: 5 minutes
Cook time: 20 minutes
Servings: 4

Ingredients

2 cups water
1 eggplant
¼ cup balsamic vinegar
½ tsp. Salt
1/2 tsp. Ground black pepper

¾ cup olive oil
2 tsps. Dark brown sugar (optional
1 tbsp. Chopped garlic

Directions

> Slice the eggplant into thin pieces.
> Place the water in your skillet, and place the steamer tray in your skillet. Bring the water to a boil, and place the eggplant on the steamer tray. Place the lid on the skillet, and steam for 20 minutes.
> While the eggplant is steaming, combine the remaining ingredient in a sealable jar. Seal the jar and shake until the ingredients are well mixed.
> Toss the steamed eggplant with the balsamic vinaigrette, salt and pepper to taste if necessary, and serve.
>

MINTY STEAMED CARROTS

Your kids will love these. The mint adds a fresh sweet flavor to the carrots, and they're oh so easy to make

Prep time: 5 minutes
Cook time: 10 minutes
Servings: 4

Ingredients

2 cups water
1 lb. Carrots
4 large fresh mint sprigs plus 1 tbsp.
Chopped fresh mint

Salt
Black pepper
1 1/2 tbsp. Butter, room temperature

Directions

> Peel the carrots.
> Place the water and mint sprigs in your skillet, and place the steamer tray in your skillet. Bring the water to a boil, and place the carrots on the steamer tray. Place the lid on the skillet, and steam for 8-10 minutes.
> Toss the steamed carrots with the chopped mint and butter, salt and pepper to taste if necessary, and serve.

SPICY SOUR STEAMED SPINACH

This recipe is fast, easy, and healthy. The apple cider vinegar gives the spinach a slightly sour flavor, and the crushed red pepper gives it some heat.

Prep time: 5 minutes
Cook time: 1 minutes
Servings: 4

Ingredients

2 cups water
1 lb. Spinach
2 tbsp. Apple cider vinegar
Salt

Black pepper
¼ tsp. Crushed red pepper

Directions

> Wash the spinach.
> Place the water your skillet, and place the steamer tray in your skillet. Bring the water to a boil, and place the spinach on the steamer tray. Place the lid on the skillet, and steam for about 1 minutes, until the spinach wilts.
> Toss the steamed spinach with the red pepper and vinegar, salt and pepper to taste, and serve.

SWEETS AND DESSERTS:

I can never say enough about this section and i won't stop now! These recipes will have you playing like a kid in the candy store. These "kiss cuddling" desserts will add a special romance to that sweet tooth you already have. This section is the best way to make up with anyone, even yourself. So snuggle up a date with one of our dazzling dessert selections. You will easily fall in love...but don't worry...they will never break your heart!

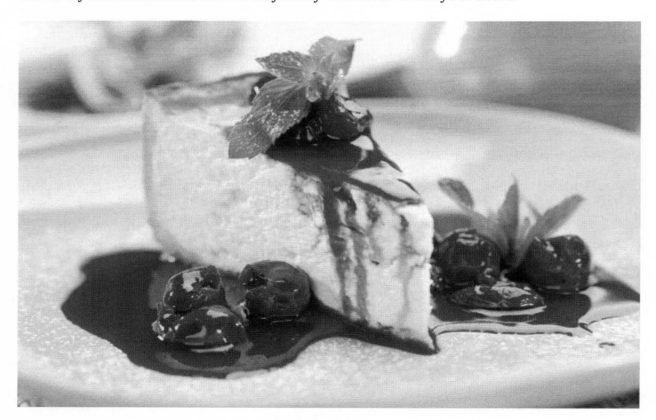

NO-SUGAR HONEY APPLE FLIPPED UPSIDE DOWN CAKE

This no-sugar apple upside down cake will satisfy your sweet tooth. The honey and molasses in the cake is often used as a substitute and is just as sweet as sugar, if not more. This is a dessert that you will want to keep making over and over again.

Prep time: 20 minutes
Cook time: 20 minutes
Servings: 8

Ingredients

1 ¾ cups all-purpose flour
1 ½ tsp. Sea salt
1 tsp. Ground cinnamon
¾ tsp. Baking soda
½ tsp. Baking powder
¾ cup mild-flavored (light) molasses

¼ cup honey
1 large egg
2 tsps. Grated peeled ginger
1/3 cup sour cream
¼ cup whole milk
3-4 peeled honey crisp or pink lady apples

Directions -

> Prepare and stir flour, salt, cinnamon, baking soda and baking powder in a mixing bowl.
> In another bowl combine honey, molasses, egg, ginger, sour cream and milk and mix thoroughly & set bowl a side. (keep a little bit of sugar and butter to caramelize apples)
> Cut apples and separate the cores. Then add apples to a non-stick skillet and cook for 3 minutes on each side along with some of the sugar and butter that you left over.
> Pour the cake batter over the top.
> Place pan in over and cook for 35 minutes at 325 degrees. (check cake with tooth pick to see if it is cooked through)
> Cool for at least 15 min and serve.
> (served best with vanilla ice cream)

Nutritional Facts:

calories (kcal) 360 , fat (g) 10 , saturated fat (g) 6 , cholesterol (mg) 55 , carbohydrates (g) 68 , dietary fiber (g) 3, total sugars (g) 39, protein (g) 4, sodium (mg) 540

THE ALL AMERICAN HONEY APPLE PIE IN A SKILLET

This isn't grandma's apple pie but believe me she wouldn't know the difference. This all american apple pie uses a refrigerated crust topped with apples, cinnamon and brown sugar. It's a dessert that will leave the whole family begging for second servings.

Prep time: 20 minutes
Cook time: 1 hour 10 minutes
Servings: 8

Ingredients

2 cups granny smith apples
2 lbs. Braeburn apples
1 tsp. Ground cinnamon
¾ cup granulated sugar
½ cup butter

1 cup brown sugar
¼ cup honey
7 oz pie crusts (refrigerated package)
1 egg white
(butter pecan ice cream if desired)

Directions

> Turn oven on and heat at 345º
> Prepare apples: peel and cut. Cover in cinnamon and sugar.
> In a non-stick skillet add brown sugar and butter. Cook until sugar is liquefied for 1 to 1 ½ minutes.
> Turn off heat and put piecrust down over the brown sugar in the pan.
> Add the apples to the piecrust and cover with the remaining piecrust.
> Add a coat of the egg whites and sugar to the top of the piecrust. (use a brush)
> Create several slits on the top for best baking results.
> Bake at 345º for about 1 hour and 15 minutes.
> Cool for at least 30 min on a towel or rack
> Best served with vanilla ice cream.

Nutritional Facts:

Serving size 232 g, amount per serving, calories 480, calories from fat 183, total fat 20.4g, saturated fat 9.4g, trans fat 0.0g, cholesterol 31mg, sodium 227mg, potassium 208mg, total carbohydrates 76.7g, dietary fiber 4.0g, sugars 59.8g, protein 2.6g

Low in cholesterol, low in sodium, very high in vitamin b6

MILK DIPPING CHOCOLATE CHIP COOKIE

You will love this recipe. No longer will you need a mixer or a cookie sheet to make cookies. You can make them all, right here, in the non-stick pan.

Prep time: 20 minutes
Cook time: 40 minutes
Servings: 4

Ingredients

3 cups all-purpose flour
1 ¼ tsp. Baking soda
1 ½ tsp. Salt
¾ cup butter, melted and cooled slightly
1 ¼ cups brown sugar

1 cup sugar
3 eggs
2 tsp. Vanilla extract
1 teaspoon cinnamon
2 ½ cups chocolate chips

Directions

> Start by heating up the oven to 350º so it is ready.
> Prepare: combine the flour, baking soda and salt in a mixing container.
> In a separate mixing container, combine butter, cinnamon and brown sugar, then add the eggs and the vanilla extract.
> Add the chocolate chips and the dry ingredients and mix together.
> Flatten the dough in a non-stick skillet and bake for 25 minutes at 325 degrees. When it starts to brown on the edges let it cook for about 5 more minutes
> Cookies will have to cool for about 15-20 min before serving...yummy!

Nutritional Facts:

Serving size 376 g, amount per serving, calories 1,623, calories from fat 629, total fat 69.9g, saturated fat 44.8g, trans fat 0.0g, cholesterol 238mg, sodium 1655mg, potassium 611mg, total carbohydrates 229.4g, dietary fiber 6.4g, sugars 148.9g, protein 22.3g

Vitamin a 28%, vitamin c 0%, calcium 28%, iron 43%, nutrition grade d-

SUMMER SWEET BERRY ECSTACY DELIGHT

For those fruit lovers out there, there is nothing better than a nice warm berry cobbler. The skillet berry delight is a cobbler in disguise and produces just the right amount of berries with a warm flaky crust.

Prep time: 10 minutes
Cook time: 10 minutes
Servings: 8

Ingredients

2 lbs. Fresh mixed berries
¼ cup plus 2 tbsps. Sugar
1 tbsps. Water
1 tbsp. Fresh lemon juice
1 cup all-purpose flour
1 tsp. Baking powder

½ tsp. Baking soda
Pinch of salt
½ cup plus 2 tbsps. Low-fat buttermilk
2 tbsps. Melted unsalted butter
1/8 tsp. Ground cinnamon mixed with 1 tsp. Sugar

Directions

> Prepare: in a mixing bowl combine the flour, baking powder. Baking soda, salt, 2 tablespoons sugar, buttermilk and butter. Create a dough.
> In a non-stick skillet add the berries with the water, lemon juice and ¼ cup of sugar.
> Cook for 15 minutes. Mix will thicken the longer you cook it.
> Spoon the dough over the fruit and season with cinnamon-sugar.
> Cover with aluminum foil and cook for 20 minutes.
> Let it cool about 15-20 min...then serve

Nutritional Facts:

Serving size 159 g, amount per serving, calories 178, calories from fat 32, total fat 3.6g Saturated fat 1.9g, trans fat 0.0g, cholesterol 8mg, sodium 137mg, potassium 253mg, total carbohydrates 33.0g, dietary fiber 4.5g, sugars 15.2g, protein 3.0g
Low in cholesterol, very high in vitamin c

SWEET TART BROWN SUGAR PEAR PIE

This tart pear pie is a perfect recipe for a perfect day. The tartness of the pie, paired with cinnamon and the doughtiness of the crust can bring anyone back to the days of their childhood.

Prep time: 10 minutes
Cook time: 40 minutes
Servings: 4

Ingredients

15 oz. Pie crust (2 9-inch unbaked pastry pie crusts)
¾ tsp. Ground ginger
1 tsp. Ground cinnamon
½ tsp. Salt
1/3 cup granulated sugar
1/3 cup firmly packed brown sugar

2 tbsp. Freshly squeezed lemon juice
1 cup heavy cream
7 fresh bartlett pears, peeled and sliced
1 large egg yolk
3 tbsp. Heavy cream
1 tsp. Light brown sugar

Directions -

> Prepare: in a mixing container, combine sliced pears, flour, ginger, cinnamon, lemon juice, cream and sugars.
> Mix butter, ¾ cup sugar for 3 minutes. Add the flour mixture and buttermilk.
> Pour the pear mixture directly into pie crust.
> In a non-stick pan add the batter over the pie crust.
> Bake at 350 for 30 minutes.. Cool and serve with ice cream and caramel sauce if desired.
> Serve with ice cream for this delicious treat! (optional)

Nutritional Facts:

Serving size 556 g, amount per serving, calories 1,043, calories from fat 484, total fat, 53.8g, saturated fat 19.1g, trans fat 0.0g

Cholesterol 109mg, sodium 894mg, potassium 565mg, total carbohydrates 137.6g, dietary fiber 13.5g, sugars 65.2g, protein 9.8g

I LOVE BUTTERMILK FRUIT PLUM CAKE SKILLET–

This is such a versatile dessert that you change it up according to season. This is a great way to ensure that your cake will never get old and that it will also be a hit at every party. Switch it up with different fruits every time you make it...it's delicious and fun!!!

Prep time: 10 minutes
Cook time: 45 minutes
Servings: 4

Ingredients

4 tbsp. Unsalted butter
1 cup all-purpose flour
½ tsp. Baking powder
¼ tsp. Baking soda
½ tsp. Salt

¾ cup sugar (plus 2 tbsp.)
1 large egg
½ cup buttermilk
2 ripe sliced medium plums

Directions

> With an electric mixture combine butter, ¾ sugar, egg, flour and buttermilk for 5 minutes.
> In a non-stick pan add the batter and arrange the plums overlapping them in rows on top with the rest of the sugar.
> Bake at 325 at 30 minutes.
> Cool and serve.

Nutritional Facts:

Serving size 219 g, amount per serving, calories 434, calories from fat 122, total fat 13.5g, saturated fat 7.9g , trans fat 0.0g, cholesterol 78mg, sodium 504mg, potassium 261mg, total carbohydrates 75.8g, dietary fiber 3.1g, sugars 48.6g, protein 6.2g
Vitamin a 8%, vitamin c 12%, calcium 8%, iron 12%, nutrition grade c+, based on a 2000 calorie diet

WARM BACKYARD S'MORE BROWNIES

S'mores have always been an indispensable dessert of the outdoors either camping or just enjoying a nice evening at home. With these blondies you can skip the fire pit and have delicious s'mores ready to eat whenever everyone is ready! Then bring them back outside for the full experience without the mess.

Prep time: 30 minutes
Cook time: 2 hours
Servings: 24

Ingredients

8 tablespoons (1 stick) unsalted butter, plus more for the pan
1 cup all-purpose flour, spooned and leveled
2 teaspoons baking powder
1 teaspoon kosher salt
1 ½ cups packed light brown sugar
2 teaspoons pure vanilla extract

2 large eggs
1 cup pecans, coarsely chopped
4 graham crackers, broken into small pieces
1 cup miniature marshmallows
1/2 cup semisweet chocolate chips
1/4 cup white chocolate chips

Directions

> Turn the oven on to 350° f. Line 9x13 baking pan with buttered aluminum foil. Mix the flour, baking powder, and salt together in a bowl.
> Melt the butter in a saucepan over medium heat. Take away from heat in order to add the brown sugar and vanilla. Beat in and combine eggs, then combine the flour mixture; lastly, add pecans.
> Evenly pour the mixture into the prepared pan and bake for 20-25 minutes. Cover the top with the graham crackers, marshmallows, and chocolate and white chocolate chips and continue to cook for 7-8 more minutes. Make sure the pan cools entirely on a wire rack. Use the foil to easily help take out the blondies. Divide into 24 bars.

Nutritional Facts:

Serving size 41 g, amount per serving, calories 178, calories from fat 85, total fat 9.4g, saturated fat 4.2g, trans fat 0.0g, cholesterol 26mg, sodium 189mg, potassium 110mg, total carbohydrates 22.1g, dietary fiber 1.0g, sugars 14.2g, protein 2.4g

BULLWINKLE'S RICH AND SMOOTH, WHIPPED CHOCOLATE TEMPTATION

Of course we're not talking about a moose, cartoon or real, but mousse: the creamy and fluffy chocolate delight. With strong coffee or espresso hints, depending on what you prefer, this tempting dessert is one of the best recipes, and also very essential to the sweet tooth's repertoire!

If you want to turn heads...make this dessert! "it's amazing!" ;)

Prep time: 1 day (optional)
Cook time: 2 hours 10 minutes (2 hours chilled)
Servings: 6

Ingredients

¾ cup chilled heavy cream, divided
4 large egg yolks
1/4 cup espresso, room temperature
1/4 tsp. Vanilla extract
3 tbsp. Sugar, divided

1/8 tsp. Kosher salt
6 oz. Semisweet chocolate (60-72% cacao), chopped
2 large egg whites

Directions

>   Whisk ½ cup cream and fluff until it forms firm tips; then cover the cream for it to chill.
>   In a metal mixing container, mix together egg yolks, espresso, vanilla extract, salt, and 2 tbsp. Sugar. Carefully place the bowl over barely simmering water, but make sure it does not come in contact with the water. Cook and continue to stir for 1 minute or until mixture has appeared to double in size and lighten in color. (you will tell that it will start to grow)
>   Take the bowl away from the pan and put in chocolate; mix until blended. Put aside until it reaches room temperature while seldom stirring so it sets correctly.
>   With the assistance of an electric mixer, beat egg white in a different bowl. Slowly add remaining sugar. Turn up speed and mix until it starts to form firm tips with the mixture.

> Fold egg whites and chocolate twice through and do the same with the whipped cream and mixture and make sure it is blended.
> Evenly split mousse and chill for 2 hours at the least. It must have time to get firm.
> Stir ¼ cup cream in a small bowl until firm tips form; spoon over mousse, serve.

Nutritional Facts:

Serving size 82 g, amount per serving, calories 252, calories from fat 154, total fat 17.1g, saturated fat 9.6g, trans fat 0.0g, cholesterol 160mg, sodium 77mg, potassium 157mg, total carbohydrates 24.8g, dietary fiber 1.7g, sugars 21.6g, protein 4.5g

Low in sodium

HEAVENLY ORANGE VANILLA ANGEL'S FOOD CAKE

Nothing is as sweet and fluffy as angel's food cake, and nothing offers more variety regarding what you're able to accompany the dessert with. Fruit, cream, chocolate, the possibilities are endless, and it allows the cook to be creative as long as the sweetness isn't overwhelmed by some odd addition; to each their own though!

Prep time: 20 minutes
Cook time: 35 minutes
Servings: 12

Ingredients

1 3/4 cups sugar
1/4 teaspoon salt
1 cup cake flour, sifted
12 egg whites (the closer to room temperature the better)

1/3 cup warm water
1/2 tsp. Orange extract
1/2 tsp. Vanilla extract
1 1/2 teaspoons cream of tartar

Directions

> Turn the oven on to 350 degrees f.
> Using an electric mixer, stir sugar for 2 minutes. At this point you want to sift together half of the sugar and combine with salt and cake flour. Put aside the extra sugar.
> In another bowl, mix and combine the egg whites, water, orange and vanilla extracts, and cream of tartar and blend well. Let sit for 2 minutes then sift in the extra sugar, continuously whisking. Sift and sprinkle flour mixture on the foam to form tips. Fold until mixture is combined.
> Using an ungreased tube pan, spread the mixture evenly. Bake for 35 minutes.
> On a wire rack, let the cake cool upside down for 1 hour at the least.
> Yummy! ;)

Nutritional Facts:

Serving size 80 g, amount per serving, calories 167, calories from fat 1, total fat 0.2g, cholesterol 0mg, sodium 84mg, potassium 128mg, total carbohydrates 37.6g, sugars 29.5g, protein 4.7g

Very low in saturated fat, no cholesterol, low in sodium

MAGNIFICENT MINI STRAWBERRY MASCARPONE INDULGENCES

Mascarpone is a soft and mild italian cream cheese and is light and sweet enough to make any dessert incredibly tasteful. When in cupcake form, the flavor is so versatile that any glaze or icing will do, and in this case, strawberry is the weapon of choice. Enjoy this great delicacy!

Prep time: 20 minutes
Cook time: 20 minutes
Servings: 48

Ingredients

8 ounces mascarpone cheese (about 1 cup), softened
2 egg whites
1/4 cup vegetable oil
1 box white cake mix

1 cup water
1/3 cup frozen strawberries, thawed and drained
2 1/2 cups powdered sugar
1/4 tsp. Vanilla extract

Directions

›   Turn on to 350 degrees f the oven to preheat. Use a mini-muffin baking tin and line each with baking cups.

›   Mix together the mascarpone cheese, egg whites, and vegetable oil together. Whisk until creamy. Mix in the water and cake mix until even with a nice creamy consistency. Fill each mini cups almost to the top and bake for 18-20 minutes (they will start to turn a golden color.) After removal, let the cupcakes cool while still in the tin for 5 minutes, then place them on a wire rack where they will sit.

›   In the meantime while cupcakes are baking, use a blender to puree the strawberries; then mix with the powdered sugar and vanilla extract in a bowl until velvety. Spread the glaze on top of each cupcake after they have completely cooled.

Note: "for the vanilla lovers!" Adding a little extra vanilla will give that little extra kiss for your taste buds! ;)

Nutritional Facts:

Serving size 30 g, amount per serving, calories 90, calories from fat 27, total fat 2.9g, saturated fat 0.8g, trans fat 0.0g, cholesterol 2mg, sodium 78mg, potassium 20mg, total carbohydrates 15.0g, sugars 12.1g, protein 1.2g

Low in cholesterol

VELVETY NO-BAKE ITALIAN HAZELNUT COCOA COOKIES

The spread most people have come to crave can be made into delicious cookie form. Mixed in with some oats and a hint of vanilla, these no-bake cookies are easy and quick to make, and sure to please the family after a good meal. Enjoy with milk if desired!

Prep time: 15 minutes
Cook time: 15 minutes
Servings: 14

Ingredients

2 cups sugar
2 tablespoons butter
½ cup milk
1 teaspoon vanilla

1/4 teaspoon powdered sugar
3/4 cup hazelnut cocoa spread
2 cups old-fashioned oats

Directions

> Use parchment paper on the cookie sheet.
> Boil 2 cups sugar, 2 tablespoons butter and 1/2 cup milk in a 4-quart saucepan over medium heat. Take off heat after 1 minute of boiling.
> Combine 1 teaspoon vanilla and 3/4 cup a hazelnut cocoa spread (a few brands out there...neutella is what i use) until well blended and soft, and then add the oats and stir until even.
> Spoon even glops onto sheet, each should be about 2 tablespoons per cookie. Sprinkle with powdered sugar after they have completely cooled.

Nutritional Facts:

Serving size 65g, amount per serving, calories 253, calories from fat 86, total fat 9.5g, saturated fat 2.8g, cholesterol 5mg, sodium 80mg, potassium 138mg, total carbohydrates 39.7g, dietary fiber 2.0g, sugars 30.5g, protein 5.3g

Very low in cholesterol, low in sodium, very high in vitamin b6

CREAMY NO-OVEN PB&C

Peanut butter and jelly is a meal, but peanut butter and chocolate make a tempting after-hours treat. Despite what many may think, both don't have to be baked and both aren't required to be unhealthy, too unhealthy that is. With the additions of reduced-fat cream cheese and greek yogurt, this is a dessert worth trying!

Prep time: 10 minutes
Cook time: 4 hours
Servings: 12

Ingredients

Crust
Cooking spray
24 chocolate wafer cookies
3 tablespoons unsalted butter, melted
2 ounces semisweet chocolate morsels, melted
2 ounces white chocolate morsels, melted

Filling
4 ounces reduced-fat cream cheese
1/2 cup creamy all-natural peanut butter
1/2 cup 2-percent greek yogurt
2/3 cup confectioners' sugar

Topping
1/4 cup chopped roasted unsalted peanuts
Kosher salt

Directions

> **Crust:** completely line an 8-inch square pan with foil that has been scarcely coated with cooking spray. Grind cookies in a food processor (a blender work as well) until crumbled fine. Melt butter and blend with the crumbs to coat. Next, melt the chocolate and mix in until pasty. Firmly spread the mixture into the bottom of the pan, and place in the refrigerator, covered.

> **Filling and topping:** clean the food processor for you will need it for making the filling. Mix together the cream cheese, peanut butter, yogurt and sugar in the processor until you see it get smooth in texture. Take the crust out of the refrigerator and spread the blended mix over the crust until it is covered evenly all over. Sprinkle the peanuts

across the top and add a pinch of salt. Re-cover and place back in the refrigerator for at least 4 hours, or for even better results, overnight.

> Loosen the mixture around the edges, and then use the foil to carefully lift it out of the pan. Divide into 12 bars and serve.

Nutritional Facts:

Serving size 230 g, amount per serving, calories 914, calories from fat 518, total fat 57.6g, saturated fat 27.4g, cholesterol 125mg, sodium 498mg, potassium 394mg, total carbohydrates 88.6g, dietary fiber 3.1g, sugars 80.0g, protein 18.0g

SOFT CLASSIC VANILLA CHOCOLATE CHIP COOKIES

Chocolate chip cookies are the most famous cookie, and certainly one of the more well-known desserts so there have been many variations along the way. So what's better than the best? The best of the best! Simple. Quick. Delightful.

Prep time: 30 minutes
Cook time: 14 minutes
Servings: 60

Ingredients

3/4 cup butter, softened
3/4 cup granulated sugar
3/4 cup firmly packed dark brown sugar
2 large eggs
1 3/4 teaspoons vanilla extract

2 1/4 cups plus 2 tbsp. All-purpose flour
1 teaspoon baking soda
3/4 teaspoon salt
1 1/2 (12-oz.) Packages semisweet chocolate morsels

Directions

> Turn oven to 350° to preheat. Mix butter and until it becomes creamy then beat in eggs and 1 1/2 tsp. Vanilla, until well blended.
> Steadily add to butter mixture (in a separate mixing container) the flour, baking soda, and salt, and mix together until smooth. Add the morsels and stir until they are evenly throughout. Scoop tablespoon-sized balls onto a baking sheet lined with parchment paper so they don't stick.
> Bake 12-15 minutes or to your liking. Place on a wire rack and let cool for at least 15 minutes.

Note: you can get creative with the things you can substitute (or combine) in this recipe for chocolate chips! A few of our favorites are: cranberries, nuts, raisins, blueberries, cherries, caramel chips, white chocolate chips!
If you have an idea for a substitute here...let us know about it! Give us a review and we may feature your recipe in our next book.

BREAKFAST:

Tired of the same old morning meals??? Well jump out of bed and jump into this chapter that is full of protein and morning munchies! We wßll turn your head with some of these! If you're not a breakfast in the morning person...then this chapter is served any time of the day! So, ladies and gentlemen...get your grub on! And "top of the morning", "afternoon" and "evening" to you, because, "breakfast is now being served!

BABY SPINACH AND GARLIC SCRAMBLED EGGS

This is an easy skillet dish for busy mornings. Here, you can combine baby spinach with your eggs for a healthy fast meal that will be a hit at the breakfast table.

Prep time: 15 minutes
Cook time: 15 minutes
Servings: 4

Ingredients

12 oz. Baby spinach leaves (package is fine as well)
½ cup chopped onion
1 clove of garlic (chopped)
4 tbsp. Heavy cream

8 eggs, beaten
Pinch of salt
Pinch of pepper
½ tsp. Dried thyme leaves
2 tbsp. Grated parmesan cheese

Directions

> Prepare: in a mixing bowl beat with eggs with cream, salt, pepper and thyme.
> Add the spinach, onion and garlic to a non-stick skillet and cook for 7 minutes.
> Pour the egg mixture to the skillet and cook for 5 minutes toss the eggs till done.
> Garnish with cheese and serve.

Nutritional Facts:

Serving size 211 g, amount per serving, calories 233calories from fat 153, total fat 17.0g, saturated fat 7.7g, trans fat 0.0g, cholesterol 355mg, sodium 279mg, potassium 636mg, total carbohydrates 6.0g, dietary fiber 2.3g, sugars 1.7g, protein 15.8g

Low in sugar, high in manganese, high in phosphorus, high in riboflavin, very high in selenium, very high in vitamin a, high in vitamin c

A PLAY ON QUICHE

This egg dish is one of my favorites. My mother used to bake many different types of quiches growing up. This is a fast and easy way to keep that traditional alive for my family.

Prep time: 10 minutes
Cook time: 10 minutes
Servings: 4

Ingredients

8 strips bacon (cut in half)
3/4 lb. Asparagus (1 bunch)
Kosher salt
Freshly ground black pepper
6 eggs

1 cup heavy cream
2 tbsp. Chopped chives
9 oz frozen puff pastry (1 sheet, thawed in refrigerator overnight)

Directions

> Prepare eggs in a mixing bowl with cream, ½ tsp. Black pepper and chives.
> Microwave bacon strips in for 3 minutes.
> In a non-stick skillet season asparagus with salt and pepper. Cook for 3 minutes, until soft.
> Roll out puff pastry on floured surface and cut into 4 equal squares.
> Place each cut out piece into 4 non-stick skillets.
> Place egg mixture, bacon and asparagus into each skillet.
> Place in the oven and bake at 350 degrees for 30 minutes.

Nutritional Facts:

Serving size 284 g, amount per serving, calories 772, calories from fat 522, total fat 58.0g, saturated fat 20.4g, trans fat 0.0g, cholesterol 328mg, sodium 1181mg, potassium 541mg, total carbohydrates 34.0g, dietary fiber 2.8g, sugars 2.6g, protein 29.6g

Low in sugar, high in selenium

COUNTRY STYLE POTATO OMELET SKILLET

Peppers, onions and ham and potatoes all in one place. Forget about flipping the perfect omelet and let the oven do all the work for you.

Prep time: 20 minutes
Cook time: 20 minutes
Servings: 4

Ingredients

8 large eggs
4 ounces diced deli ham
2 diced bell peppers
1 diced onion
1 tsp. Kosher salt

1 tsp. Freshly ground pepper
2 tbsp. Unsalted butter
3 cups frozen shredded hash browns
4 ounces grated smoked gouda cheese
1/2 cup scallions (chopped)

Directions

> To prepare the eggs, add them to large mixing bowl and whisk them until foamy.
> In a non-stick skillet add the ham, bell peppers, onions, salt and pepper and cook for 6 minutes.
> Add to the bowl with eggs.
> Add the hash browns to the skillet and cook for 5 minutes.
> Pour the egg mixture over the hash browns and then add the skillet to the oven.
> Cook for 4 minutes.
> Add the cheese and scallions and cook for 2 more minutes.
> Garnish with scallions and serve.

Nutritional Facts:

Serving size 382 g, amount per serving, calories 686calories from fat 367, total fat 40.8g, saturated fat 14.8g, cholesterol 436mg, sodium 1770mg, potassium 1132mg, total carbohydrates 51.0g, dietary fiber 6.4g, sugars 7.1g, protein 29.1g

High in selenium, very high in vitamin c

ITALIAN STYLE EGGS AND PANCETTA

Making eggs into comfort food? Adding pancetta, basil and sauce to these eggs will remind you of mom's cooking minus the meatballs.

Prep time: 35 minutes
Cook time: 35 minutes
Servings: 4

Ingredients

1 diced medium onion
2 chopped cloves of garlic
1 oz. Chopped pancetta
2 cups prepared marinara sauce
4 large eggs

6 large fresh basil leaves, torn into small pieces
1 tbsp. Grated parmesan cheese
¼ tsp. Freshly ground pepper
4 toasted slices whole-wheat country bread

directions

> In a non-stick skillet combine onion, garlic and pancetta. Cook for 5 minutes.
> Add marinara sauce and bring down to a simmer.
> Crack an egg and gently add it to the skillet.
> Season with basil, cover and cook for 8 minutes.
> Garnish with cheese and pepper and serve with bread.

Nutritional Facts:

Amount per serving, calories 314, calories from fat 117, total fat 13.0g, saturated fat 4.1g, trans fat 0.2g, cholesterol 199mg, sodium 914mg, potassium 622mg, total carbohydrates 32.7g, dietary fiber 5.8g, sugars 14.2g, protein 16.4g

High in niacin, high in selenium

HOMESTYLE BACON PEPPER POTATO BREAKFAST FILLER

When you can't choose between sausage or bacon, toast or muffins. This breakfast skillet has it all.

Prep time: 45 minutes
Cook time: 45 minutes
Servings: 4

Ingredients

2 lbs. Potatoes (cubed)
½ lb. Bacon

1 bell pepper (diced green)
1 teaspoon crushed red peppers

Directions -

> -in a pot bring potatoes to boil; cooking for 12 minutes.
> - in a non-stick skillet cook the bacon for 5 minutes. Set aside when finished.
> Add potatoes to the pan and stir in peppers, onion, crushed red peppers and mushrooms. Cook for 5 minutes. (making sure they start to turn a little brown)
> Stir in bacon, cover with cheese and cook eggs together til eggs are done cooking & set.
> Garnish and serve.
> Cook eggs to your preferred style. Place potatoes in a large serving dish, and top with the eggs.
> Serve while it's hot!

Nutritional Facts:

Amount per serving, calories 474, calories from fat 217, total fat 24.1g37%, saturated fat 7.9g, trans fat 0.0g, cholesterol 62mg, sodium 1325mg, potassium 1315mg, total carbohydrates 38.5g, dietary fiber 6.2g, sugars 3.9g, protein 25.1g

Low in sugar, high in selenium, very high in vitamin c

SPICY BACON AND HASH BROWN POTATOES SKILLET

This skillet adds a little heat to your palate. By combining chilies in the dish, you have decided to kick it up a notch, especially in the flavor scale.

Prep time: 30 minutes
Cook time: 30 minutes
Servings: 4

Ingredients

¾ lb. Chopped bacon
3 cups hash brown potatoes (refrigerated cooked shredded)
3 large eggs

4oz green chilies (1 can)
¾ cup shredded cheddar cheese
1 chopped medium tomato

Directions

> Prepare eggs in a mixing bowl with chilies.
> In a non-stick skillet cook bacon for 7 minutes.
> Add potatoes and cook for 10 more minutes.
> Pour eggs over potatoes and cook for 10 minutes.
> Add cheese and tomato, cover and cook for 2 more minutes. When cheese is melted...it's done!
> Garnish and serve.

Nutritional Facts:

Amount per serving, calories 924, calories from fat 549, total fat 61.0g, saturated fat 19.5g, trans fat 0.0g, cholesterol 255mg, sodium 2664mg, potassium 1298mg. Total carbohydrates 46.0g, dietary fiber 4.1g. Sugars 3.9g, protein 45.3g

Low in sugar, high in selenium

FOR THE LOVE OF SEASONED BREAKFAST POTATOES SKILLET

If you love potatoes, especially for breakfast, then this is the recipe for you. This recipe was created for the spud lover and wanted to bring it to the main stage.

Prep time: 40 minutes
Cook time: 40 minutes
Servings: 6

Ingredients

5 russet potatoes (peeled)
1 ½ tsp. Kosher salt
¼ tbs. Freshly ground black pepper

1 cup scallions (2 bunches diced)
1 tsp. Sea salt (coarse)

Directions

> Season potatoes with salt and pepper.
> Place half of the potatoes in a non-stick skillet, add scallions and top with more potatoes.
> Cook for 12 minutes.
> Flip over and cook for 12 more minutes.
> Garnish with sea salt and scallions and serve.

Nutritional Facts:

Amount per serving, calories 129, calories from fat 2, total fat 0.2g, cholesterol 0mg, sodium 907mg, potassium 772mg, total carbohydrates 29.3g, dietary fiber 4.8g, sugars 2.4g, protein 3.3g

Very low in saturated fat, no cholesterol, high in dietary fiber, high in potassium, high in vitamin b6, very high in vitamin c

BLISSFUL B.L.T. BISCUITS

The famous b.l.t. is no longer just dedicated to lunch. Bacon is already used in breakfast, can be in every other meal truthfully, and tomatoes and kale (our lettuce substitute) are just as adaptable. Add an egg and stick in between a sliced biscuit and you have a great start to your day!

Prep time: 10 minutes
Cook time: 30 minutes
Servings: 8

Ingredients

1 can (16.3 oz) pillsbury™ grands!™
homestyle refrigerated buttermilk biscuits
8 slices thick-cut maple bacon
1/4 cup packed brown sugar

8 pasteurized eggs*
1 handful fresh kale leaves
1 large avocado, pitted, peeled and sliced
1 large tomato, cut into 8 slices

Directions

> Preheat oven to 325°f and use a cookie sheet that is not greased. Place on the sheet a can of refrigerated buttermilk biscuits, the sides are allowed to touch so don't worry about them touching. Bake in oven until biscuits start to turn golden brown, which can range anywhere from 22-24 minutes.

> Raise the oven to 400°f and place the bacon strips on foil atop a cookie sheet. In a separate mixing container, mix together the brown sugar with a tablespoon of water and then coat each slice of bacon. Bake until crisp, about 20 minutes, then use paper towels or something to sop up or drain the bacon.

> Next it's time to bring the sandwiches together. Slice open each biscuit, splitting evenly across the middle.

> You may cook the eggs to your liking.

> Work in layers from the bottom biscuit up: kale leaves, avocado, tomato, egg, then bacon. Put the top biscuit on and you're sandwich is ready.

> This is what you call "breakfast, lunch or dinner!" Yummm... ;)

Nutritional Facts:

Serving size 113 g, amount per serving, calories 246, calories from fat 86, total fat 9.6g, saturated fat 1.4g, trans fat 0.0g, cholesterol 1mg, sodium 622mg, potassium 329mg, total carbohydrates 36.3g, dietary fiber 1.4g, sugars 7.0g, protein 4.6g

Very low in cholesterol, high in phosphorus, very high in vitamin a, very high in vitamin c

A BUNNY'S FLUFFY BREAKFAST DELIGHT

The old cliché is that rabbits enjoy carrots, but they aren't the only ones, especially when offered in cake form. These cookie bars are hearty and full of great ingredients balance out the "cake" /"cookie" label: apples, raisins, & oats! The doc would approve.

Prep time: 20 minutes
Cook time: 40 minutes
Servings: 14

Ingredients

1 package refrigerated sugar cookies
1 3/4 cups quick-cooking oats
1/2 cup cranberry raisins.
1 teaspoon ground cinnamon

3/4 cup chopped carrots (1 medium)
2 cups chopped honey crisp apples
2 eggs

Directions

> Bring refrigerated sugar cookies to room temperature.
> Preheat oven to 375° f. Make sure to use cooking spray on the sheet pan.
> After breaking up the cookie dough, mix in oats, cranberry raisins, and ground cinnamon until blended in a mixing container.
> Using the pulse option on a food processor, beat the chopped carrots for 15-20 seconds then add the apples and beat for another 10-15 seconds.
> Break the eggs into the cookie dough mixture then add the carrots and apples. Mix very well before placing all of the batter into pan.
> Bake in oven for 30 minutes. Afterwards, let stand for 10 minutes in order to cool.

Nutritional Facts:

serving size 79 g, amount per serving, calories 166, calories from fat 24, total fat 2.7g, saturated fat 0.6g, trans fat 0.0g, cholesterol 23mg, sodium 289mg, potassium 122mg, total carbohydrates 30.3g, dietary fiber 2.6g, sugars 3.8g, protein 5.3g
Low in saturated fat, high in manganese, high in selenium, high in vitamin a, high in vitamin b6

SWEET AND SOFT FRENCH TOAST FINGERS

Cinnamon, vanilla, maple syrup, and yogurt; there's not much else to say except for the fact that these french toast sticks will be a hit with the entire family. There is a double dose of ingredients with the toast and the sauce so there will be plenty of flavor to go around!

Prep time: 5 minutes
Cook time: 4 minutes
Servings: 2

Ingredients
4 eggs
½ cup vanilla nonfat greek yogurt
1/4 tsp. Powdered sugar
¼ tsp. Ground cinnamon
4 slices wide-loaf day-old bread

Sauce
¾ cup vanilla nonfat greek yogurt
¼ cup pancake syrup
1/8 tsp. Ground cinnamon

Directions
> Create sauce by combining greek yogurt, pancake syrup, and cinnamon.
> Using a separate dish, beat eggs and blend in yogurt, powdered sugar, and cinnamon.
> Slice each piece of bread into 4 sticks. Immerse each side of each stick in the egg mixture.
> Heat nonstick skillet over medium heat. Cook each bread stick, in batches if necessary, for 1-2 minutes on each side, reducing the heat slightly if needed. There should be no liquid remains visible. If needed, clean the skillet between batches.

Nutritional Facts:
Serving size 299 g, amount per serving, calories 377, calories from fat 101, total fat 11.2g, saturated fat 4.4g, trans fat 0.0g, cholesterol 337mg, sodium 385mg, potassium 502mg, total carbohydrates 45.3g, dietary fiber 0.6g, sugars 21.0g, protein 21.2g

High in phosphorus, high in riboflavin, high in selenium

PEPPERY MINCED GARLIC HOME FRIES ON THE STOVE

Nothing beats a hearty home-cooked meal, and considering breakfast is the most important meal of the day and usually consumed at home, there is good reason to begin your day with energy from classic home fries. Potatoes, onions, and spices will get you going in no time!

Prep time: 20 minutes
Cook time: 20 minutes
Servings: 4

Ingredients

1 1/2 pounds russet potatoes (about 3 medium or 2 large potatoes)
2 tablespoons olive oil, divided
1 tablespoon unsalted butter
1 medium onion, diced

2 cloves minced garlic
1 teaspoon smoked paprika
1 teaspoon parsley
Pinch of salt
Pinch of pepper

Directions

> Cut the washed potatoes into half-inch squares. Cover with cold water in a saucepan and season with a pinch of salt. After the water boils, cook for 1-2 minutes or until soft.
> Add 1 tablespoon of olive oil in a skillet over medium heat and cook the onions and garlic for 5 minutes, occasionally stirring, using season salt and pepper to season.
> After draining the potatoes, let stand for 5 minutes to cool.
> Add the remaining olive oil and butter in another skillet over medium heat. Season the potatoes with salt and pepper and toss them around in the oil, then cook them for 8-10 minutes, spreading them out in the pan. Batches are suggested depending on the size of the skillet or size of the cubes.
> Mix in the cooked onions and garlic, parsley, and paprika to the skillet and continue mixing the potatoes.
> Serve immediately after turning off the heat ands removing the pan.

Note: to make this a special treat...sprinkle a little cheese over top of potatoes and let stand 5 min till cheese melts. Mmmmmmm ;)

Nutritional Facts:

Serving size 213 g, amount per serving, calories 219, calories from fat 92, total fat 10.2g, saturated fat 2.9g, cholesterol 8mg, sodium 614mg, potassium 760mg, total carbohydrates 30.4g, dietary fiber 5.0g, sugars 3.2g, protein 3.4g

Good points, low in cholesterol, very high in vitamin c

MOIST & HEARTY OATMEAL BLUEBERRY MUFFINS

Blueberry muffins are very recognizable in the breakfast world, very simple, and very popular despite their humbleness. They never were really missing anything, but to add a little more substance, oats provide an extra kick to this already appealing course!

Prep time: 20 minutes
Cook time: 1 hour & 45 minutes
Servings: 12

Ingredients
1 1/2 cups all-purpose flour
1 cup quick-cooking oats
2 1/4 teaspoons baking powder
1 teaspoon coarse salt
1/2 teaspoon ground cinnamon
3/4 cup sugar

2 large eggs
1 stick unsalted butter, melted and cooled
1/2 cup whole milk

1 cups blueberries
1/4 cup cranberries

Directions
> Preheat oven to make sure oven is warm, at 350 degrees. Place baking cups into a 12-cup baking tray.
> Mix together flour, oats, baking powder, salt, and cinnamon in a mixing container.
> Using a different mixing container, mix together sugar, eggs, butter, and milk.
> Combine both mixtures, then add blueberries and cranberries to the blend.
> Fill each cup a quarter of the way up, and keep even if there is extra batter. Bake for 20 minutes. Let the muffins sit in the pan for 5 minutes before removing and transferring to wire rack to cool entirely.
> Note: sprinkle a few pinches of brown sugar and a drop of vanilla on top of each muffin before putting them in the oven! "a sure way to make you smile!" ;)

FRESH OMELETTES, OH MY!

Omelets are a breakfast and brunch basic, and they are incredibly easy to make! Besides being simple and classic, the breakfast dish is also very versatile and a variety of ingredients can be used to cook up what you crave the most. Onions, peppers, mushrooms, cheese, scallions, pepperoni, whatever you want, you can't go wrong.

Prep time: 15 minutes
Cook time: 15 minutes
Servings: 1

Ingredients
2-3 eggs
Salt and pepper, to taste
2 cloves minced garlic

1/4 cup chopped onion
2-3 tsp. Butter (can use less with nonstick pan)

Directions
> Beat the 2-3 eggs and season as desired.
> Add butter to a fry pan over medium to medium-high heat. Make sure the bottom and sides are coated as it melts. Then add the egg mixture . Allow the eggs to set up for 30 sec; sliding the pan back & forth very gently. Let it set for just another min.
> Lift the edge of the egg mixture carefully with spatula and slant the pan, allowing the liquid on top to touch the surface of the pan. (you can also use a fork or something flat to achieve this result) repeat this step around the entire omelet making sure the eggs are set up evenly around the omelet. If the omelet is moving around easily, but staying together, it's ready.
> With this pan it should be very easy to slide right out of the pan! ;)

Nutritional Facts:
Serving size 132 g, amount per serving, calories 214, calories from fat 148, total fat 16.4g, saturated fat 7.6g, cholesterol 348mg, sodium 180mg, potassium 187mg, total carbohydrates 5.4g, dietary fiber 0.8g, sugars 2.0g, protein 11.9g
High in riboflavin, very high in selenium

SAVORY SUPERFOOD FRITTATA

This is primarily a breakfast dish, but is easy enough to make for lunch or dinner, however, let's get the day started off right. Another superfood emerges in kale, and though sweet potato may seem like an odd addition to breakfast, it blends perfectly with this tasty dish!

Prep time: 20 minutes
Cook time: 10 minutes
Servings: 4

Ingredients

6 large eggs
1 c. Half-and-half
1 tsp. Kosher salt
½ tsp. Freshly ground pepper
1/4 tsp. Cinnamon
2 c. Sweet potatoes

2 tbsp. Olive oil
1 c. Spinach (firmly packed chopped)
1 c. Kale (firmly packed chopped)
½ small red onion
2 clove garlic
3 oz. Goat cheese

Directions

> Combine the eggs, half-and-half, salt, pepper, and cinnamon after you preheat the oven to 350 degrees f.
> Add 1 tablespoon oil to a nonstick skillet over medium and sauté potatoes for 8-10 minutes. After removal, cover them with foil to keep warm. Using the same skillet, cook spinach, onion, and garlic in another tablespoon of oil for 3-4 minutes; add the potatoes back in and pour the egg mixture over everything. Cook for 3 minutes then dust the top with goat cheese.
> Bake 10-14 minutes and you're all ready to go.
> Quick, tasty and fun for everyone! ;)

Nutritional Facts:

Serving size 276 g, amount per serving, calories 447calories from fat 263, total fat 29.2g, saturated fat 12.9g, trans fat 0.0g, cholesterol 324mg, sodium 805mg, potassium 948mg, total carbohydrates 28.2g, dietary fiber 3.9g, sugars 1.9g, protein 19.8g

Low in sugar, high in vitamin a, high in vitamin c

THE ESSENTIAL TOASTED BREAKFAST SANDWICH

Simple is probably the most underrated characteristic in recipes. Sometimes we just need to get back to basics because the best lies within. Bacon, eggs, cheese, and toast all in one! Fruit makes the perfect garnish, and everything you need is right in front of you (coffee optional, if needed).

Prep time: 4 minutes
Cook time: 6 minutes
Servings: 2

Ingredients
2 eggs
2 tbsp. Milk or water
3 tsp. Butter, room temperature, divided
4 slices bread of choice

2 slices cheese of choice
4 slices fully-cooked bacon
1/4 tsp. Basil

Directions
> Whish together eggs, milk, salt and pepper.
> Melt 1 teaspoon butter in a large nonstick skillet over medium heat. Add the egg mixture, and carefully mix back and fourth with a spatula just for a minute, just until they start to set up. Cook until thick and there is no visible liquid to the eggs & there is no stirring necessary. Clean the skillet before the next step.
> Butter one side of each slice of bread. Grill the bread, buttered side against the surface of the skillet, top each with scrambled eggs, cheese and bacon. Put the other slices of on top of the ingredients, with the buttered side up this time.
> Cook 2-4 minutes, flipping the sandwich halfway through.
> Makes a yummy treat for breakfast, lunch or dinner… ;)

Nutritional Facts:
Serving size 225 g, amount per serving, calories 737, calories from fat 412, total fat 45.8g, saturated fat 19.4g, trans fat 0.0g, cholesterol 272mg, sodium 2095mg, potassium 491mg, total carbohydrates 39.6g, dietary fiber 1.8g, sugars 4.4g, protein 39.7g

Ceramic Titanium Cookbook

Low in sugar, high in selenium, total fat: 23 g, saturated fat: 11 g, polyunsaturated fat: 2 g, monounsaturated fat: 6 g, cholesterol: 239 mg, sodium: 698 mg, carbohydrates: 24 g, dietary fiber: 4 g, protein: 23 g

Vitamin a: 777.6 iu, vitamin d: 52.7 iu, folate: 52.7 mcg, calcium: 256.9 mg, iron: 2.4 mg, choline: 156.7 mg

GETTING FRIED UP!

Throw it in the fryer and "drop it like it's hot!" Frying food has never been easier! These recipes will have you crunching away with the techniques of this frying basket. The grease falls back into the pan after pulling the food up when it's ready! Savory dishes seasoned to perfection and more than plenty to go around! Hope you have just as much fun as we did as you master your craft and show your friends that you have skills in the kitchen! Enjoy!

DEEP FRIED OREOS

This might sound like a weird thing to do to oreos, but they're delicious. They're best served hot sprinkled with some powdered sugar.

Prep time: 5 minutes
Cook time: 5 minutes
Servings: 52 cookies (about 8 servings)

Ingredient
2 cups bisquick
2 eggs
1 ½ cups milk

3 teaspoons oil
6 cups vegetable oil
1 (20 ounce) package oreo cookies

Directions
> Pour the vegetable oil in a non-stick skillet and heat until the oil reaches 375 f.
> Mix together the first 4 ingredients until smooth.
> Put the oreos in the mix until completely covered in batter.
> Place the battered oreos in the skillet and fry until the bottom turns brown, and then flip the oreos over.
> Allow the oreos to cool for a couple minutes before serving.

Nutritional Facts:

Serving size 8 (321g), calories 1951, total fat 185.1g, saturated fat 36.9g, trans fat 3.8g, cholesterol 45mg, sodium 743mg, potassium 220mg, total carb 71.1g, dietary fiber 2.7g, sugars 34.3g, protein 8.9g

CRISPY DEEP FRIED TOFU

This makes a great crunchy appetizer. It has a slight nutty flavor from the sesame seeds, and goes well with plum sauce.

Prep time: 15 minutes
Cook time: 5 minutes
Servings: 24 pieces (about 6 servings)

Ingredients

1 lb firm tofu, cut into 1 inch squares and dried
1/3 cup sesame seeds
2 tablespoons cornstarch
3 tablespoons flour

1/4 teaspoon sugar
1/4 cup vegetable oil
Salt and pepper to taste

Directions:

> Combine the cornstarch, flour, sesame seeds, and sugar.
> Heat the oil on medium heat
> While the oil is heating, cover the tofu completely with the cornstarch mixture.
> Fry the tofu until it turns brown
> Allow the tofu to drain on a plate lined with paper towels, and salt and pepper to taste.
> Serve with plum sauce.

Nutritional Facts:

Serving size 6 (109g), calories 216, total fat 16.4g, saturated fat 3.1g, trans fat 0g, cholesterol 0mg, sodium 1842mg, potassium 213mg, total carb 11.8g , dietary fiber 3g, sugars 0.7g, protein 8.5g

MOJO POTATOES

Mojos are thick cut fried potato wedges. They're always a huge hit as a side dish or appetizer.

Prep time: 10 minutes
Cook time: 5 minutes
Servings: 4-6

Ingredients:

1/2 cup flour
1 teaspoon garlic salt
3/4 teaspoon pepper
1/4 teaspoon celery salt
1/4 teaspoon salt

4 medium potatoes, unpeeled but cleaned
1 egg, beaten
6 cups vegetable oil

Directions:

> Combine the flour and seasoning.
> Slice the potatoes into wedges that are ½ inch thick.
> Heat the oil to 375 f.
> Coat the wedges with the beaten egg, and then coat them with the flour mixture.
> Fry for about 5 minutes until the potatoes are golden.
> Drain on a plate lined with paper towels.
> Serve with your favorite sauce.

Nutritional Facts:

Serving size 6 (379g), calories 2076, total fat 219g, saturated fat 43.1g, trans fat 0g, cholesterol 27mg, sodium 117mg, potassium 608mg, total carb 30.8g, dietary fiber 3.8g, sugars 1.8g, protein 4.5g

DEEP FRIED ICE CREAM

Rolling the ice cream in corn flakes allows you to fry it without melting. The ice cream has a nice crunchy outside, and soft ice cream center.

Prep time: 1 hour
Cook time: 15 seconds
Serving: 8

Ingredients

1/2 gallon ice cream
2 beaten eggs
2 -3 cups crushed corn flakes
1 teaspoon cinnamon

1/2 cup honey
2 cups whipped cream
6 cups vegetable oil

Directions:

> Shape the ice cream into balls about the size of baseballs. Then allow them to harden in the freezer for a short time.
> Coat them with the egg then coat them with the corn flakes. Allow the balls to harden in the freezer again.
> Heat the oil to 375 f.
> Dip the balls in the oil, and let them fry for 15 seconds.
> Fry for about 5 minutes until the potatoes are golden.
> Drain on a plate lined with paper towels and top with cinnamon.

Nutritional Facts:

Serving size 8 (243g), calories 1660, total fat 174.3g, saturated fat 38.5g, trans fat 0g, cholesterol 76mg, sodium 129mg, potassium 77mg, total carb 28.8g, dietary fiber 0.7g, sugars 19.1g, protein 2.9g

LOUISIANA SOUTHERN FRIED BREAD

This is an old southern favorite. It goes great with soup, and chili. You can also top it with your favorite ingredients for a thick taco.

Prep time: 1 hour
Cook time: 10 minutes
Servings: 3-4

Ingredients

1 cup flour
1 tablespoon sugar
1 teaspoon baking powder
1/4 teaspoon salt

1/2 cup cold water
6 cups vegetable oil

Directions:

> Combine all the ingredients except for the oil. Let them rest for at least an hour. A dough will form.
> Heat the oil to 375 f.
> Oil your hands and form the dough into 3 or 4 pieces.
> Fry the pieces for about 5 minutes a side until it turns golden.
> Drain on a plate lined with paper towels and serve.

Nutritional Facts:

Serving size 4 (393g), calories 3017, total fat 327.3g, saturated fat 64.2g, trans fat 0g, cholesterol 0mg, sodium 150mg, potassium 160mg, total carb 27.4g, dietary fiber 0.9g, sugars 3.1g, protein 3.2g

FRIED RICE CAKES

This is an old new orleans favorite. They have a nice sweet flavor. They're great for a sweet treat, or as part of your breakfast.

Prep time: 15 minutes
Cook time: 25 minutes
Servings: 3-4

Ingredients

6 tablespoons flour
3 tablespoons sugar
2 teaspoons baking powder
1/4 teaspoon salt
1/4 teaspoon vanilla

2 cups cooked rice
2 eggs
1 pinch nutmeg
6 cups vegetable oil
Powdered sugar

Directions:

> Combine the first 5 ingredients.
> Combine the eggs and rice in a different bowl.
> Combine the 2 mixtures in the bowl that contains the rice.
> Heat the oil to 360 f in your skillet.
> Fry spoonfuls of the of the rice mixture until it turns golden brown. It should take a few minutes.
> Drain on a plate lined with paper towels and top with powdered sugar and nutmeg.

Nutritional Facts:

Serving size 4 (494g), calories 3450, total fat 330g, saturated fat 65.1g, trans fat 0g, cholesterol 82mg, sodium 186mg, potassium 402mg, total carb 121.5g, dietary fiber 1.6g, sugars 37.1g, protein 10.6g

FRIED RAVIOLI

This makes a great bite sized appetizer. Serve them with a side of marinara, pesto, or arrabiata sauce.

Prep time: 15 minutes
Cook time: 15 minutes
Servings: 4-6

Ingredients

3 cups olive oil for frying
1 cup buttermilk
2 cups italian style breadcrumbs
20 ounces cheese ravioli (about 24 ravioli)

1/4 cup parmesan cheese, freshly grated 9 ounces favorite italian sauce, heated, for dipping

Directions:

> Heat the oil to 325 f in your skillet.
> While the oil is heating, put the buttermilk and breadcrumbs in two separate bowls. Coat the ravioli with the buttermilk. Let the extra buttermilk drip off the ravioli. Then coat with the bread crumbs
> Fry the ravioli in batches, until golden, about 3 minutes.
> Drain on a plate lined with paper towels and top with cheese.
> Serve with a side of your favorite italian sauce.

Nutritional Facts:

Serving size 6 (279g), calories 1121, total fat 105.5g, saturated fat 16.3g
Trans fat 0g, cholesterol 14mg, sodium 550mg, potassium 332mg, total carb 43.5g dietary fiber 2.8g, sugars 8.1g, protein 10.1g

FABULOUS FRIED CHICKEN

This isn't traditional fried chicken, it's spiced with sage. It has a delicious flavor, and makes a great choice for picnics.

Prep time: 1 hour
Cook time: 20 minutes
Servings: 4-6

Ingredients

3 lbs chicken, cleaned and cut into pieces
1 cup buttermilk
1/2 cup flour
1 teaspoon salt
1/2 teaspoon ground sage
1/4 teaspoon paprika

1/4 teaspoon pepper
2 eggs, beaten with
1 tablespoon water
1 cup breadcrumbs
6 cups peanut oil

Directions:

> Make sure the chicken is dry, and place it in a shallow dish.
> Add the buttermilk to the dish with the chicken, and let it rest for 30 minutes. Turn the chicken a couple times during the 30 minutes
> While the chicken is marinating place the breadcrumbs and eggs in 2 separate bowls
> Mix the spices in a large plastic bag, and add in the chicken. Shake the bag until the chicken is completely coated with the spices.
> Coat the chicken with the egg then coat it with the breadcrumbs.
> Allow the chicken to rest for another 15 minutes.
> While the chicken is resting, heat the oil in your skillet to 375 f.
> Fry the legs and thighs for 10 to 12 minutes. Then add the remaining pieces of chicken, and fry for an additional 10 minutes.
> Drain chicken on a plate lined with paper towels, and served.

HONEY GLAZED FRIED MANCHEGO CHEESE

The honey gives a sweet flavor to the saltiness of the cheese. Frying the cheese gives it a nice crunchy texture.

Prep time: 20 minutes
Cook time: 5 minutes
Servings: 4

Ingredients
1 cup all-purpose flour
1 egg, lightly beaten
1 cup panko breadcrumbs
1/2 lb manchego cheese, cut into 1 1/2-inch cubes

6 cups canola oil
Honey
Smoked paprika

Directions:
> Put the first 3 ingredients in separate bowls.
> Coat the cheese with the flour, then egg, and then breadcrumbs.
> Heat the oil in skillet to 375f on medium heat.
> Fry the cheese in batches. Fry the cheese until it turns golden, no more than 5 minutes.
> Drain cheese on a plate lined with paper towels.
> Drizzle with honey, and top with paprika. Serve immediately.

Nutritional Facts:
Serving size 4 (686g), calories 1386 total fat 350g, saturated fat 69.4g, trans fat, cholesterol 84mg, sodium 686mg, potassium 585mg, total carb 30.4g, dietary fiber 6.2g, sugars 2.7g, protein 9.8g

AVOCADO FRIES

The batter gives the mild flavored avocado a nice kick. The breading makes this fries nice and crunchy, with a soft center,

Prep time: 10 minutes
Cook time: 5 minutes
Servings: 4

Ingredients

6 cups vegetable oil (for frying)
2 avocados cut into 1/4 inch strips
1 cup flour
1 teaspoon cumin
1 teaspoon coriander

1 teaspoon salt
1 teaspoon white pepper
2 eggs
1/2 cup milk
1 cup panko breadcrumbs

Directions:

> Mix the flour and seasoning together. Place the breadcrumbs in a separate bowl.
> Lightly beat the milk and egg together.
> Coat the avocado with the flour, then milk mixture, and finally the breadcrumbs
> Heat the oil in skillet to 375f on medium heat.
> Fry the avocado until it turns golden, no more than 5 minutes.
> Drain the avocado on a plate lined with paper towels.
> Serve with your favorite dipping sauce.

Nutritional Facts:

Serving size 4 (522g), calories 1286 total fat 350g, saturated fat 69.4g, trans fat, cholesterol 84mg, sodium 686mg, potassium 585mg, total carb 40.4g, dietary fiber 8.5g, sugars 2.3g, protein 9.8g

GETTING STEAMY IN HERE!

It's just like being at the gym in the steam room, but this time it will be the food that you are steaming! These recipes give a whole new meaning to the words "steaming!" We went out of our way to pack the punch into these super steamy recipes so you can enjoy every pleasurable, and succulent bite! Follow the directions and you have a "win-win" situation! Great for locking in the vitamins in those veggies! Enjoy!

SIMPLY STEAMED SNOW CRAB LEGS

This recipe is fast, and only has one ingredient. Steaming the crab legs allows all of their sweet flavor to come alive

Prep time: 3 minutes
Cook time: 14 minutes
Servings: 4

Ingredients
2 cups water
2 lbs. Snow crab leg

Directions
> Wash the ice off of the crab legs.
> Place the water your skillet, and place the steamer tray in your skillet. Bring the water to a boil, and place the crab legs on the steamer tray. Place the lid on the skillet, and steam for about 6-14 minutes, until the crab is completely cooked.
> Serve the crab with dipping sauce of your choice.

Nutritional Facts:
Serving size 4 (345g), calories 220, total fat 3.5g, saturated fat 0.3g, trans fat 0g, cholesterol 120mg, sodium 1891mg, potassium 595mg, total carb 0g, dietary fiber 0g, sugars 0g, protein 43.9g

STEAMED EGGS

Steaming the eggs makes them softer and easier to peel. Steam the eggs for 10 minutes if you like a softer yolk

Prep time: 3 minutes
Cook time: 12 minutes
Servings: 1-2

Ingredients
2 cups water
2 eggs

Directions
> Allow the eggs to come to room temperature.
> Place the water your skillet, and place the steamer tray in your skillet. Bring the water to a boil, and place the eggs on the steamer tray. Place the lid on the skillet, and steam for about 6-14 minutes, until the eggs are completely cooked.
> Allow the eggs to cool for about 15 minute, and then run under cold water before opening the eggs.

Nutritional Facts:
Serving size 2 (281g), calories 63, total fat 4.4g, saturated fat 1.4g, trans fat 0g, cholesterol 164mg, sodium 69mg, potassium 61mg, total carb 0.3g, dietary fiber 0g, sugars 0.3g, protein 5.5g

CHILI LIME STEAMED HALIBUT

The chili lime dressing gives the delicate halibut a spicy and tangy flavor. The herbs add an aromatic tropical flavor.

Prep time: 5 minutes
Cook time: 11 minutes
Servings: 4

Ingredients:
For the dressing
3 limes, juice of
1 teaspoon kosher salt
1 tablespoon sugar
1 teaspoon oyster sauce
1 garlic clove, roughly chopped (if you're a garlic lover(add more)
1/2 teaspoon fresh ginger, roughly chopped

1/2 teaspoon chili sauce (or hot sauce)
For the fish
1 lb halibut fillet (or other white fish, sufficient for four servings)
3 ounces of fresh mint
1 tablespoon fresh thai basil
1 tablespoon fresh cilantro

Directions
> Put all the dressing ingredients in a blender & puree til smooth. Add more salt if needed.
> Place the water your skillet, and place the steamer tray in your skillet. Bring the water to a boil, and place the halibut on the steamer tray. Place the lid on the skillet, and steam for about 11 minutes, until the halibut is completely cooked.
> While the halibut is steaming, chop the basil, cilantro, and mint
> Cover the cooked halibut with the dressing, and then top with the chopped herbs.

Nutritional Facts:
Serving size 124g, amount per serving, calories 75, calories from fat 2, total fat 0.9g, cholesterol 7mg, sodium 65mg, potassium 120mg, total carbohydrates 47g, dietary fiber 9g, sugars 8g, protein 12g

WASABI STEAMED BROCCOLI

The wasabi butter transforms this dish from ordinary to extraordinary. The wasabi butter gives the broccoli a rich and spicy flavor

Prep time: 3 minutes
Cook time: 5 minutes
Servings: 4

Ingredients:
1 head broccoli
2 cups water

1 tablespoon softened butter
2 teaspoon wasabi powder

Directions
> Cut the broccoli into pieces.
> Place the water your skillet, and place the steamer tray in your skillet. Bring the water to a boil, and place the broccoli on the steamer tray. Place the lid on the skillet, and steam for about 5 minutes, until the broccoli is completely cooked.
> While the broccoli is steaming mix the butter and wasabi powder
> Toss the cooked broccoli with the wasabi butter and serve.

Nutritional Facts:
Serving size 157g, amount per serving, calories 81, calories from fat 6, total fat 0.7g, cholesterol 0mg, sodium 197mg, potassium 434mg, total carbohydrates 16.7g, dietary fiber 3.9g, sugars 4.2g, protein 3.8g

ASIAN STEAMED SALMON

The soy sauce and ginger give the salmon a salty and spicy flavor. The soy sauce also allows you to cut out any added salt.

Prep time: 3 minutes
Cook time: 5 minutes
Servings: 4

Ingredients:

1 lb salmon fillet, cut into 4 pieces (1-1/4 lbs and 1/2 to 3/4-inch thick)
2 teaspoons low sodium soy sauce
3 tablespoons scallions, finely chopped

2 teaspoons fresh gingerroot, minced
1/8 teaspoon ground black pepper

Directions

> Place the water your skillet, and place the steamer tray in your skillet. Bring the water to a boil, and place the salmon with the skin side on the steamer tray. Use a brush to coat the top of the salmon with 1 teaspoon of soy sauce. Top with about a tablespoon of scallions. Place the lid on the skillet, and steam for about 5 minutes, until the salmon is completely cooked.
> Put the salmon with the skin side down on to a plate
> Top with the remaining soy sauce, scallions, ginger, and pepper.

Nutritional Facts:

Serving size 124g, amount per serving, calories 75, calories from fat 2, total fat 0.9g, cholesterol 7mg, sodium 65mg, potassium 120mg, total carbohydrates 47g, dietary fiber 9g, sugars 8g, protein 12g

STEAMED VEGGIES WITH CHARMOULA SAUCE

This is an easy to make, healthy side dish. Charmoula sauce comes from the middle east and is packed with tons of flavor.

Prep time: 20 minutes
Cook time: 15 minutes
Servings: 6

Ingredients:

1 lb green beans, ends trimmed
1/2 lb carrot, trimmed into sticks the same thickness as beans
1 large garlic clove, slightly chopped
1 cup cilantro, coarsely chopped
1/2 cup flat leaf parsley, coarsely chopped

3 tablespoons olive oil
2 tablespoons lemon juice
1/2 teaspoon smoked paprika
1/2 teaspoon ground cumin
Salt & freshly ground black pepper
2 cups water

Directions

> Place the water your skillet, and place the steamer tray in your skillet. Bring the water to a boil, and place the carrots on the steamer tray. Place the lid on the skillet, and steam for about 3 minutes, and then add the beans, and cook for another 5 minutes.
> While the vegetables are steaming put the garlic, cilantro, and parsley in a food processor, and pulse until finely chopped. Add the remaining ingredients and pulse until well combined. Salt and pepper to taste.
> Toss the cooked vegetables with half of the sauce, and the top with the remaining sauce. Add more salt and pepper if necessary, and serve.

Nutritional Facts:

Serving size 124g, amount per serving, calories 75, calories from fat 2, total fat 0.9g, cholesterol 7mg, sodium 65mg, potassium 120mg, total carbohydrates 47g, dietary fiber 9g, sugars 8g, protein 12g

HONEY STEAMED PEARS

This is a great dessert especially when you want to try something different. You can substitute white wine if you don't have cognac.

Prep time: 5 minutes
Cook time: 10 minutes
Servings: 4

Ingredients:

4 pears cut in half, seeds and core removed
4 tablespoons honey
4 tablespoon cognac
2 cups water

Directions

> Put the honey and cognac in the middle of half of the pieces of pear, and cover with the remaining pieces.
> Place the water your skillet, and place the steamer tray in your skillet. Bring the water to a boil, and place the pears on the steamer tray. Place the lid on the skillet, and steam for about 10 minutes, until the pears is completely cooked.
> Serve the pears hot.

Nutritional Facts:

Serving size 175, amount per serving, calories 98, calories from fat 5, total fat 0.7g, cholesterol 0mg, sodium 194mg, potassium 120mg, total carbohydrates 16.7g, dietary fiber 3g, sugars 4g, protein 3g

STEAMED VEGGIES WITH HONEY SAGE DRESSING

The lemon gives some tanginess to this sweet dish. The sage gives it a nice woodsy flavor

Prep time: 10 minutes
Cook time: 15 minutes
Servings: 4-6

Ingredients:

1/4 lb sweet potato, peeled,and cut into chunks
1/4 lb snow peas
1/4 lb yellow squash, cut into 1 inch slices
1/4 lb new potato
1 ounce lemon juice (add to water for steaming)
1/2 teaspoon honey

2 tablespoons fresh lemon juice
1 tablespoon balsamic vinegar
1/8 cup minced sweet onion
1 tablespoon toasted sesame seeds
1 tablespoon minced fresh sage
1/8 teaspoon crushed dried coriander
2 cups water

Directions

> Place the water and 1 ounce lemon juice in your skillet, and place the steamer tray in your skillet. Bring the water to a boil, and place the vegetables on the steamer tray. Place the lid on the skillet, and steam for about 15 minutes
> While veggies are steaming mix together the remaining ingredients to make the dress.
> Toss the cooked vegetables with the dressing, and serve.

Nutritional Facts:

Serving size 157g,, calories 81, calories from fat 6, total fat 0.7g, cholesterol 0mg, sodium 197mg, potassium 434mg, total carbohydrates 31g, dietary fiber 5g, sugars 6g, protein 18g

SOY STEAMED RED SNAPPER

This sauce gives the snapper a delightful sweet and spicy flavor. The best part is it's quick and easy to make.

Prep time: 10 minutes
Cook time: 10 minutes
Servings: 4

Ingredients:

1 lb red snapper fillet
1 tablespoon light soy sauce
1 tablespoon sugar
1 teaspoon fresh ginger, finely grated

1 garlic clove, minced
1/8 teaspoon black pepper
1/8 teaspoon salt
2 cups water

Directions

> Mix together all the ingredients except for the fish.
> Brush the fish with sauce
> Place the water in your skillet, and place the steamer tray in your skillet. Bring the water to a boil, and place the fish on the steamer tray. Place the lid on the skillet, and steam for about 10 minutes. Brush the fish with the sauce occasionally while steaming.
> Serve immediately.

Nutritional Facts:

Serving size 124g,, calories 62, calories from fat 2, total fat 0.9g, cholesterol 2mg, sodium 98mg, potassium 120mg, total carbohydrates 48g, dietary fiber 9g, sugars 8g, protein 12g

STEAMED YELLOW SQUASH WITH ONIONS

This recipe is simple, but delicious. The butter, salt, and pepper let the flavor of the vegetables take center stage.

Prep time: 5 minutes
Cook time: 15 minutes
Servings: 4-5

Ingredients:

5 yellow squash, washed and quartered   *Salt*
1/4 cup butter   *Black pepper*
1 vidalia onion, chopped coarsely

Directions

> Place the water in your skillet, and place the steamer tray in your skillet. Bring the water to a boil, and place the squash on the steamer tray. Place the lid on the skillet, and steam for about 5 minutes.
> Melt the butter on medium-high heat in a saucepan. Then add in the onions and cook until translucent. Put in the squash and combine. Salt and pepper to taste.
> Serve immediately.

Nutritional Facts:

Serving size 157 g, calories 81, calories from fat 6, total fat 0.7g, cholesterol 0mg, sodium 197mg, potassium 434mg, total carbohydrates 16.7g, dietary fiber 3.9g, sugars 4.2g, protein 3.8g,

LEMON STEAMED SALMON

After biting into this delicious dish you will think it was expressed to your door straight from alaska! This salmon is perfectly moist and has a great lemon flavor. Best of all it's quick and easy to make., yummy for your tummy and plenty to share! Dig in! :)

Prep time: 5 minutes
Cook time: 4 minutes
Servings: 2

Ingredients

2 cups water
1 cup white wine
2 2 oz. Salmon fillets
1 bay leaf
1 tsp. Salt

1/2 tsp. Ground black pepper
1 tbsp. Black peppercorns
4-8 lemon slices

Directions

> Place the water, wine, bay leaf, and peppercorns in your skillet, and place the steamer tray in your skillet. Bring the water to a boil, and place the lemon slices on the steamer tray then place the salmon on top of the lemon, salt and pepper to taste. Place the lid on the skillet, and steam for 4 minutes.

> Serve the salmon with the side dish of your choice.

Nutritional Facts:

Serving size 124g,, calories 75, calories from fat 2, total fat 0.9g, cholesterol 7mg, sodium 65mg, potassium 120mg, total carbohydrates 47g, dietary fiber 9g, sugars 8g, protein 12g

KEEPIN IT "CRISPY!"

Crispy is what crispy does! If you like it crispy and are on the healthy side of town, then these crisper recipes will have you jumping in the air shouting "amen!" Crispy...try super crispy! Anything you put in this crisper is almost like cooking with an air fryer. And if there is fat in the food you are cooking then the grease drips down to the pan below, keeping it from touching the food you eat! "now that's what i call amazing technology in the kitchen!" Enjoy!

Sasha Hassler/Allison August

HONEY DIJON PIGS IN A BLANKET WITH TANGY MUSTARD SAUCE

These are an easy appetizer to make or the perfect finger food when you're using the bbq. They've got a delicious depth of flavor thanks the mustard.

Prep time: 15 minutes
Cook time: 15 minutes
Servings: 4-6

Ingredients:

1 8 ounce can of cresecent rolls
Mustard sauce:
¼ cup dijon mustard
½ cup sour cream
20 mini hot dogs or cocktail franks

½ cup mayonaise
1 egg, lightly beaten
3 tablespoons dijon mustard
1 tablespoon whole-grain
Mustard

Directions

> Preheat your oven to 350f.
> Slice each piece of dough into 3 equal pieces lengthwise.
> Lightly coat the dough with the dijon with a brush, and place a hot dog in each piece of dough. Make sure the hot dogs are put on one side of the dough and roll the dough around the hot dogs.
> Place the rolled up hot dogs in your crisper. Make sure the seam side is down, and brush with the beaten egg. Add poppy seeds or sesame seeds to the top if desired.
> Bake for around 12-15 minutes. They will be golden brown when ready.
> While the pigs in a blanket are cooking, mix all the dip ingredients in a bowl. Refrigerate the dip until it's time to serve the pigs in a blanket.
> Serve the pigs in a blanket hot.

Nutritional Facts:

Serving size 6 (473g), calories 550, total fat 18.2g, saturated fat 6g, trans fat 2g, cholesterol 4200mg, sodium 630mg, potassium 400mg, total carb 80.2g, dietary fiber 4.9g, sugars 16.8g, protein 30.7g

GARLIC FLAVORED BACON CHEESEY FRIES

There's nothing better than french fries, except when you add bacon and cheese. The best part is there's no oil used so they're healthier

Prep time: 5 minutes
Cook time: 25 minutes
Servings: 3

Ingredients

3 strips cooked bacon
½ cup shredded cheese

1 package frozen fries
1 tbsp. Garlic powder

Directions

> Preheat your oven to 400 f.
> Put the fries in a single layer in the crisper and bake for 15-20 minutes. They will be golden brown when finished
> Preheat your broiler
> Sprinkle the cheese on the fries and top with bacon. Sprinkle the garlic powder over the top of the cheese. Broil for 1-2 minutes until the cheese melts.
> Serve immediately.

Nutritional Facts:

Serving size 3 (473g), calories 625, total fat 14.3g, saturated fat 4.7g, trans fat 0g, cholesterol 500mg, sodium 568mg, potassium 605mg, total carb 49.6g, dietary fiber 4.9g, sugars 12.2g, protein 28.6g

MELTED MOZZARELLA STUFFED ONION RINGS

You get double the delight with this recipe. They're a delicious combo of onion rings and mozzarella sticks.

Prep time: 1 hour 30 minutes
Cook time: 22 minutes
Servings: 3

Ingredients:

1 large sweet onion, cut into 1/2 inch thick rings
2 1/2 cups buttermilk
12 sticks part skim mozzarella cheese sticks, frozen
1 cup whole wheat flour, divided ¾ cup and ¼ cup
3 large eggs beaten

1/2 cup cornmeal
1/2 cup panko
1/2 cup corn chex or cornflakes, crushed
1/2 teaspoon kosher salt
1/4 teaspoon ground black pepper
Marinara sauce or ranch dressing, for dipping

Directions

> Put the onions and buttermilk in shallow container and refrigerate for a minimum of an hour. Make sure the onions are coated by the buttermilk.
> Preheat your oven to 425f. Use aluminum foil to line a baking sheet.
> Put the onions on the baking sheet. Place them in couples. Make sure that one onion is ½ smaller than the other. Place the smaller one inside the larger one.
> Take the string cheese out of the freezer and let it soften for 5 minutes. Slice the cheese into quarters lengthwise. Put a piece of cheese in space between the two onions.
> Put ¾ cup flour in a small sized bowl. Have the eggs in a second bowl. Mix the remaining flour, panko, chex, cornmeal, salt, and pepper in a third bowl.
> Dip the onion rings in the pure flour bowl, then egg, then pure flour again, before putting it in the eggs again. Then dip the onion rings in the seasoning bowl.
> Put the onion rings in a single layer in your crisper and bake for around 22 minutes.
> Serve immediately with marinara or ranch if desired.

Nutritional Facts:

Serving size 3 (473g), calories 609, total fat 17.3g, saturated fat 5.7g, trans fat 0g, cholesterol 500mg, sodium 967mg, potassium 709mg, total carb 80.3g, dietary fiber 4.9g, sugars 14.8g, protein 32.7g

SPICY MAPLE SYRUP TWICE BAKED SWEET POTATOES

These make a great side dish, or dessert. The cayenne gives a little heat to this sweet dish

Prep time: 15 minutes
Cook time: 1 hour 20 minutes
Servings: 12

Ingredients:

9 sweet potatoes, about 12 ounces each
1 tablespoon canola or vegetable oil
1 stick (8 tablespoons) unsalted butter, cut into tablespoons
1/3 cup pure maple syrup, ideally grade b

3/4 teaspoon ground cinnamon
Salt
Cayenne pepper
3 cups mini marshmallows

Directions

> Preheat your oven to 350 f.
> Use a fork to prick the sweet potatoes 5 or 6 times all over. Then bake them for around 1 hour. The will be tender when done.
> Allow the potatoes to cool a little. Then slice them in half lengthwise. Take out the flesh and put it in a saucepan. Keep 12 of the potato skins. Put the saucepan on medium heat, mash and whip the potatoes with a whisk for about 5 minutes. Add in the butter, maple syrup, cinnamon, cayenne, and salt. Continue to whisk until smooth & mixture is hot.
> Put the mixture in the 12 potato skins. Place them in your crisper, and push the marshmallows into the top of the potatoes. Bake for another 15 minutes, then turn on the broiler until the top of the marshmallows are browned, about 1 minutes.
> Serve immediately.

Nutritional Facts:

Serving size 12 (336g), calories 615, total fat 9.7g, saturated fat 5.3g, trans fat 0g, cholesterol 20mg, sodium 1039mg, potassium 2150mg, total carb 124.2g, dietary fiber 11.2g, sugars 41g, protein 4.3g

PARMESAN CRUSTED BAKED ZUCCHINI

This makes a perfect appetizer or side dish. The parmesan gives these a nice crunch, and the oregano gives them a nice woodsy flavor.

Prep time: 10 minutes
Cook time: 40 minutes
Servings: 4-6

Ingredients:
2 medium zucchini sliced into 1/8 inch thick rounds
2 tablespoons melted butter

1 tablespoon fresh oregano
1/4 cup grated parmesan cheese

Directions
> Preheat your oven to 350 f.
> Mix the zucchini with the butter and oregano.
> Place the zucchini in your crisper and top with parmesan. Bake for 40 minutes.
> Salt and pepper to taste.

Nutritional Facts:
Serving size 6 (100g), calories 167, total fat 12.1g, saturated fat 7.9g, trans fat 0g, cholesterol 37mg, sodium 384mg, potassium 162mg, total carb 3.7g, dietary fiber 0.9g, sugars 1g, protein 13g

BAKED CHICKEN PARM

This dish is easy and quick to make. The best part is you get all the chicken parm taste without the fat from frying.

Prep time: 5 minutes
Cook time: 30 minutes
Servings: 6

Ingredients:

¾ cup plain breadcrumbs
½ teaspoon italian seasoning
¼ teaspoon garlic powder
6 boneless skinless chicken breasts

1 egg beaten
1 jar marina sauce
1 cup shredded mozzarella cheese

Directions

> Preheat your oven to 350 f.
> Mix together the seasoning, garlic powder, and breadcrumbs in a dish. Dip the chicken in the egg and then the breadcrumb mixture. Place the chicken in your crisper.
> Bake the chicken for 20 minutes. Then coat with marina and top with cheese, and bake for 10 additional minutes.
> Serve immediately with pasta if desired.

Nutritional Facts:

Serving size 6 (302g), calories 306, total fat 11.2g, saturated fat 2g, trans fat 0g, cholesterol 99mg, sodium 589mg, potassium 469mg, total carb 21.6g, dietary fiber 3.2g, sugars 8.7g

BAKED LEMON THYME CHICKEN WINGS

These wings have a great citrus flavor that mixes well with the woodsy flavor of the thyme. The best part is there's very little prep time.

Prep time: 15 minutes
Cook time: 20 minutes
Servings: 8

Ingredients:

*4 pounds chicken wings, cut in half at joint
(wing tips removed)
1/4 cup fresh lemon juice
1 tablespoon ground pepper
1 tablespoon garlic powder
1 tablespoon onion powder*

*2 teaspoons coarse salt
2 teaspoons dried thyme crushed
1/2 teaspoon cayenne pepper
1/4 cup (1/2 stick) unsalted butter, melted
Blue cheese or ranch dressing, or barbecue
sauce, for dipping*

Directions

> Preheat your oven to 500 f.
> Toss the lemon juice and chicken in a big bowl. Then mix in the pepper, thyme, salt and pepper, garlic powder, and onion powder. Then mix in the bitter and cayenne.
> Place the chicken wings in your crisper in a single layer. Bake the chicken for 30 minutes.
> Serve immediately with sauce of your choice.

Nutritional Facts:

Serving size 8 (246g), calories 492 , total fat 22.7g, saturated fat 8.3g, trans fat 0g
Cholesterol 217mg, sodium 719mg, potassium 594mg, total carb 2.2g, dietary fiber 0.4g
Sugars 0.8g, protein 66.1g

BAKED SPICY GARLIC RANCH CHICKEN STRIPS

These strips are packed with flavor. The ranch makes them tangy, the cayenne gives them heat, and the garlic gives them a nice aromatic flavor.

Prep time: 35 minutes
Cook time: 20 minutes
Servings: 3-4

Ingredients:

12 chicken tenders
1 cup ranch dressing
1 tbsp milk
1 cup complete baking mix
1/2 tsp paprika
1/2 tsp salt

1/2 tsp black pepper
1/2 teaspoon cayenne pepper
2 garlic cloves minced
Blue cheese or ranch dressing, or barbecue sauce, for dipping

Directions

> Preheat your oven to 475 f.
> Put the chicken and ranch in a large resealable plastic bag and shake it until the chicken is completely coated. Refrigerate the chicken for 30 minutes.
> Place the remaining ingredient in another large resealable plastic bag and then add in the chicken. Shake the bag until the chicken is fully coated with the seasoning.
> Put the chicken in your crisper in a single layer, and bake for 20 minutes, or until baked through.
> Serve immediately with dipping sauce of your choice.

Nutritional Facts:

Serving size 4 (424g), calories 606 , total fat 22g, saturated fat 5.9g, trans fat 0g, cholesterol 253mg, sodium 1042mg, potassium 705mg, total carb 11.9g, dietary fiber 0.6g, sugars 2.8g, protein 84g

BAKED ADOBO LIME STEAK FAJITAS

Adobo is a puerto rican seasoning mix that is packed with exotic flavor. It pairs well with the citrus flavor with the lime.

Prep time: 35 minutes
Cook time: 20 minutes
Servings: 3-4

Ingredients:

1 lb. Thin sirloin steak, slice in 1/4 inch strips
1 white onion sliced
1 red bell pepper, sliced
1 green bell pepper, sliced

1 tbsp oil
3 tsp adobo
Juice from 2 limes
Flour or white corn tortillas

Directions

> Preheat your oven to 400 f.
> Place the oil, adobo, and lime juice in a bowl and mix well. Then toss the steak and vegetable in the mixture
> Place the ingredient in your crisper in a single layer. Bake for 20 minutes
> Serve immediately with tortillas

Nutritional Facts:

Serving size 4 (248g), calories 405, total fat 16.6g, saturated fat 4g, trans fat 0g, cholesterol 101mg, sodium 216mg, potassium 659mg, total carb 22.5g, dietary fiber 4.2g, sugars 5.2g, protein 37.5g

BAKED CAJUN "SQUARE PAN FRIED" FISH STRIPS

This is a kiced up version of the fish from fish and chips. The cajun seasoning, and the garlic add a world of flavor. Yum!

Prep time: 10 minutes
Cook time: 15 minutes
Servings: 4

Ingredients:

1 1/2 pounds skinless, boneless pollock (or other firm white fish), cut into 2-by-4-inch pieces
2 3/4 cups crispy rice cereal, crushed
3 teaspoons cajun seasoning

2 garlic clove finely minced
Kosher salt
Black pepper
3 large eggs

Directions

> Preheat your oven to 450 f.
> Mix together the cereal, garlic, seasoning, and pepper in a bowl.
> Whisk the eggs with a pinch of salt, until the mixture becomes frothy.
> Dip the fish in the egg mixture and then the cereal mixture.
> Place the fish in your crisper and bake until the fish is cooked through, around 15 minutes.
> Serve immediately, with fries if desired.

Nutritional Facts:

Serving size 4 (132g), calories 265, total fat 7.8g, saturated fat 2.2g, trans fat 0.4g, cholesterol 168mg, sodium 3045mg, potassium 314mg, total carb 33.5g, dietary fiber 2.2g, sugars 8.8g, protein 16.9g

"BONUS SECTION" MARINADES!

10 HAND SELECTED MOUTHWATERING MARINADES FOR MEATS:

If you want your meat to be an amazingly "high flavored, smack in the mouth" taste that you've never experienced before...then we have **"this bonus section"** for you! These are our 10 favorite marinades that we pulled out of "our play book" just for you! Every pulsating taste of bliss that you'll every want on your meat is right here at your fingertips! Someone once asked me if i marinade my meats! My response was..."absolutely!" This is a regular practice for me and i take pride in this process. My theory on this one is..."if you have a piece of meat, then it better be soaking in some delicious juices that will have you begging for more. Now...take your meal and "dive in head first" to these delicious meat soaking juices! ;)

APPLE CIDER HOT MUSTARD GARLIC MARINADE:

Ingredients:

1/2 cup apple cider vinegar
1/2 cup dry mustard
4 tbsp. Of garlic juice

1/3 cup sugar
1 egg
1 cup mayonnaise

Directions:

> Combine all of these ingredients, except the garlic and mayonnaise, in a blender for best results!
> Prepare and warm up these ingredients in a pan on medium heat.
> You will start to see the sauce get thicker.
> After it thickens from the heat mix in 4 tbsp. Of garlic juice 1 cup mayonnaise and stir the mixture!

CINNAMON BASIL HONEY MARINADE WITH GARLIC

Ingredients:

1/2 cup onion (minced)
1/4 cup fresh lemon juice
1/4 cup avocado oil
2 tbsp. Low sodium soy sauce
2 cloves garlic (crushed or minced)

1 tbsp. Ginger (grated fresh)
2 tbsp. Honey
1/2 tsp. Cinnamon
1 tsp. Basil
2 tsp. Chopped fresh parsley

Directions:

> Combine all of these ingredients together in a blender for best results!

WHITE WINE JALAPEÑO/CAYENNE MARINADE

Instructions:

2 1/2 cups white wine (dry)
1/2 teaspoon cayenne pepper
1 jalapeno pepper (minced)
1 teaspoon onion powder

1/2 cup soy sauce
1/2 teaspoon garlic powder
1/2 tsp. Parsley
1/2 tsp. Fresh ground pepper

Directions:

> Combine all of these ingredients together in a blender for best results!

RED WINE SWEET CAJUN MARINADE

Instructions:

1/3 cup soy sauce & 1/2 cup red wine
2 tablespoons cajun seasoning
2 tablespoons minced garlic
2 tablespoons brown sugar

1/2 teaspoon cinnamon
1 tablespoon tomato paste
1 teaspoon freshly ground black pepper
1 splash of lemon juice

Directions:

> Combine all of these ingredients together in a blender for best results!

LEMON PEPPER BASIL MARINADE

Ingredients:

2/3 cup lemon juice
3 oz water
2 teaspoons chicken bouillon (granules)

2 cloves garlic (minced)
1 teaspoon pepper (fresh ground)
1/2 teaspoon basil

Directions:

> Combine all of these ingredients together in a blender for best results!

MOUTH WATERING MEXICAN STYLE MARINADE

Ingredients:

1/4 cup lime juice
1/4 cup avocado oil
1/3 cup water
1 tablespoon vinegar
2 teaspoons soy sauce (low sodium)
2 teaspoons worcestershire sauce
1 clove garlic, minced

1/2 teaspoon chili powder
1/2 teaspoon beef bouillon paste
1/2 teaspoon ground cumin
1/2 teaspoon cilantro
1/2 teaspoon dried oregano
1/4 teaspoon ground black pepper

Directions:

> Combine all of these ingredients together in a blender for best results!

PINEAPPLE RASPBERRY MEAT TWISTER MARINADE

Ingredients:

1/2 cup raspberry preserves
1/2 teaspoon lemon juice
1/2 cup pineapple juice
1/2 cup soy sauce

2 tablespoons rice vinegar
1/2 teaspoon minced garlic
1/2 teaspoon dried basil

Directions:

> Combine all of these ingredients together in a blender for best results!

ITALIAN MEAT MARINATING MAGNIFIER

Ingredients:

1/2 cup italian dressing
1/2 teaspoon lemon juice
1/2 teaspoon minced garlic

1/2 teaspoon dried basil
1/2 teaspoon tobasco sauce

Directions:

> Combine all of these ingredients together in a blender for best results!

MILD MARINADE SEAFOOD SOAKER

Instructions:

1/2 cup onion (minced)
1/4 cup fresh lemon juice
1/8 cup avocado oil

1/8 cup butter (almond butter best)
2 tsp. Chopped fresh parsley

Directions:

> Combine all of these ingredients together in a blender for best results!

WHITE WINE SEAFOOD GARLIC MARINADE

Instructions:

2 1/2 cups white wine (dry)
1/8 cup avocado oil
1 tbsp. Old bay seasoning

1/4 cup fresh lemon juice
2 tsp. Chopped parsley (fresh)
2 tsp. Paprika

Directions:

> Combine all of these ingredients together in a blender for best results!

DID YOU APPRECIATE THIS PUBLICATION? HERE'S WHAT YOU DO NOW...

If You Were Please With Our Book Then Please Leave Us A Review! In The World Of An Author Who Writes Books Independently, Your Reviews Are Not Only Touching But Important So That We Know You Like The Material We Have Prepared For "YOU" Our Audience! So Leave Us A Review…We Would Love To See That You Enjoyed Our Book!

If For Any Reason That You Were Less Than Happy With Your Experience Then Send Me An Email At **Feedback@Healthylifestylerecipes.Org** And Let Me Know How We Can Better Your Experience. We Always Come Out With A Few Volumes Of Our Books And Will Possibly Be Able To Address Some Of Your Concerns. Do Keep In Mind That We Strive To Do Our Best To Give You The Highest Quality Of What "We The Independent Authors" Pour Our Heart And Tears Into.

Again…I Really Appreciate Your Purchase And Thank You For Your Many Great Reviews And Comments! With A Warm Heart! ~Sasha Hassler & Allison August…Xoxo :)

A LITTLE ABOUT THE AUTHORS OF THIS BOOK

Sasha Hassler & Allison August are A Highly Trained, Self Taught, Private Gourmet Chef That Has Enjoyed Her Craft In The Kitchens Of Many Celebrities And Exclusive Events Of Southern California. She Enjoys Creating New Recipes For An Array Of Categories And Writes Recipes And Books From Their Heart And Soul To Share With You!

WANT FREE BOOKS?

OUR NEW BOOKS SENT TO YOUR EMAIL MONTHLY

If you were pleased with our book then you can **go to amazon where you purchased this book and <u>leave us a good review!</u>** In the world of an author who writes books independently, your reviews are not only touching but important so that we know you like the material we have prepared for "you" our audience! So leave us a review...we would love to see that you enjoyed our book!

If for any reason that you were less than happy with your experience then send me an email at **<u>feedback@healthylifestylerecipes.org</u>** and let me know how we can better your experience. We always come out with a few volumes of our books and will possibly be able to address some of your concerns. Do keep in mind that we strive to do our best to give you the highest quality of what "we the independent authors" pour our heart & tears into.

Again...i really appreciate your purchase and thank you for your many great reviews and comments! With a warm heart!
<u>www.healthylifestylerecipes.org/freebook2review</u>

OTHER BOOKS WE HIGHLY RECOMMEND!

A second must have book that we highly recommend is **our cuisinart 3-in-1 burger press cookbook! "monster burger recipes!"** This book is packed with some amazing ways to "burger your burgers!" Over 99 reasons to be the life of the party and control those bragging rights. After you try some of these "mile high" burgers you will never go back to the old way it was done in the past! So check this book out for yourself and grab one for your friends! It makes a great gift and even a better surprise!: link below!
www.Amazon.Com/Cuisinart-Burger-Press-Cookbook-Entertainment/Dp/1539557685

A Third Classic Book That We Highly Recommend Is **Our Presto Electric Skillet Cookbook! You Can Do The "Electric Slide" With These Recipes** Because They Are Nonstick And Slide Around In The Pan! This Book Will Show You How To Cut That Electric Bill In Half By Turning On That Electric Skillet And Whipping Up Some Of Those Savory Delicious Meals That Are Featured In This Easy To Make Recipe Book. We.Ve Got You Covered On All Types Of Meals You Can Make With This Skillet. This Recipe Book Will Show You How To: Stir Fry, Sauté, Bake, Warm And Even Whip Up Some Of The Most Delicious Desserts, "Just Like Grandma Used To Make!" Just Check It Out!
www.Amazon.Com/Our-Presto-Electric-Skillet-Cookbook-Ebook/Dp/B01N46QL1T

Our last recommendation is **our kitchenaid ice cream recipe book. "tickle your taste buds!"** With these impulsive, flavored recipes to get that alternative **dessert deliciousness!** We show you how to get the most out of your kitchen aid ice cream maker by stuffing this book with the most **impressive ice cream, sorbet, frozen yogurt, gelato and milkshake's** that are very easy to make, simple & sweet, yummy & tasty, but **"sinfully delicious & creative!"** For your friends, family...or that special someone...w can make **incredibly healthy desserts!** This amazing book even has a **one-of-a-kind exclusive adult section** for those who dare to spike desserts creatively! ;)
www.Amazon.Com/Kitchenaid-Cream-Maker-Recipe-Book/Dp/154283614X

Made in the USA
Middletown, DE
01 July 2017